THORSONS ORGANIC WINE GUIDE

Jerry Lockspeiser and Jackie Gear
– with Alan Gear –

Foreword by Tim Atkin

Thorsons
An Imprint of HarperCollins*Publishers*

Thorsons
An Imprint of GraftonBooks
A Division of HarperCollins*Publishers*
77—85 Fulham Palace Road,
Hammersmith, London W6 8JB

Published by Thorsons 1991
1 3 5 7 9 10 8 6 4 2
© 1991 Jerry Lockspeiser and Jackie Gear

Jerry Lockspeiser and Jackie Gear assert the moral right to
be identified as the authors of this work

A CIP catalogue record for this book
is available from the British Library

ISBN 0-7225-2451-X

Typeset by Harper Phototypesetters Limited,
Northampton, England
Printed in Great Britain by
Mackays of Chatham, Kent

CONTENTS

ACKNOWLEDGEMENTS

A guide by its very nature depends to a large extent on the co-operation of those who are 'responsible' for the individual entries. This book is no exception, and we would like to thank all of those who so freely gave of their time to provide us with the information we requested. We are particularly indebted, though, to vignerons Guy Bossard and Georges Hubert Dutel, who provided valuable insights into the Gallic scene and helped us to get to grips with organic vineyard practices. Elsewhere, Mark Richardson of Organics brought us up to date with what is happening in Italy, whilst Roy Cook of Sedlescombe Vineyard, Sussex, helped with information on organic grape growing in less favoured areas! We would also like to thank Gillian Pearkes of the English Vineyards Association.

As to the mechanics of putting the book together, we were greatly helped by Neil Smith and Adrian Sims of Prompt Computers at Leamington Spa who set up the database for collating the information in Part 2.

It is a common courtesy in books to refer to the support given by long-suffering spouses. In this case it is especially apposite since Alan Gear was drafted in at an early stage to help with checking entries and proof-reading. We should also like to thank Christine Bailey of the Henry Doubleday Research Association, for typing the frequently illegible manuscript, speedily and with great patience.

Finally, we would like to say that any mistakes are entirely down to us. Inevitably in the time that has elapsed between writing and publication some wines may have ceased to be available, some vintages may have changed or some may have gone up in price. We would like to apologize in advance for any inconvenience that may be caused because of this.

Jerry Lockspeiser   Jackie Gear
Vinceremos Wines   Henry Doubleday Research Association

FOREWORD

by Tim Atkin, Wine Correspondent for *The Guardian*

As I settle down to write this, the party conference season has just ended. For all three major political groupings, environmentalism has jostled its way to the top of the political agenda. This is a dramatic turnaround. Only five years ago, so-called green issues were considered cranky — to be lumped together with alternative medicine and ley lines.

After a decade of rampant individualism, our politicians have at last begun to realize that collective action is the only way to save the planet. As the journalist Christopher Hitchens has written: 'The values of solidarity, collectivism and internationalism are not so much desirable as they are actually mandated by nature and reality itself.'

It may seem a long way from the ozone layer to organic wines, but the distance is shorter than it appears. Each of us can contribute to a healthier world. Buying lead-free petrol, boycotting aerosols and supporting organic viticulture are all small, but significant, political acts.

No one should buy organic wines solely for ideological reasons: they don't have to. The quality of organic produce has increased enormously in the last decade. Organic wines have proved that they can stand comparison with some of the most famous châteaux and estates in the world.

Why don't people buy more organic wine, then? Part of the problem is classification. There is no one definition of organic wine; a single EC directive would clear up the confusion. As things stand, there are dozens of organic associations (the best known are Terre et Vie, Nature et Progrès, Vida Sana, Suolo e Salute and the Bundesverband Okologischer Weinbau), and each has its own regulations.

All of these associations are committed to organic winemaking and viticulture, but their interpretations vary. All eschew artificial fertilizers and synthetic pesticides, but some allow copper sulphate spraying against mould. The level of sulphur dioxide permitted in the winery also varies.

Thorsons Organic Wine Guide surveys the associations, looks at additives (both legal and illegal) and tells you which chemicals are potentially dangerous. This is serious stuff. The London Food Commission has found 49 carcinogenic compounds in the sprays winemakers use against vine diseases and 61 that may cause birth defects.

The increasing availability of organic wines, beers, spirits and juices is a testament to their acceptance by the consumer. Supermarkets don't stock unpopular wines for long. Safeway have led the way in the high street, followed by the Co-op and Asda. We are also fortunate to have a number of excellent specialist suppliers in Britain, such as Vintage Roots, Vinceremos and Haughton Fine Wines. This guide will help you to distinguish between them.

Reductions in sulphur dioxide (which can cause headaches and shortness of breath) are a good thing. So (in a broader sense) is organic farming: cutting down on the use of insecticides, fungicides and artificial fertilizers. As one American winemaker put it recently: 'The bottom line is: if we can grow grapes organically and produce equal or superior fruit, then why not do it? Quality is the key; not just quality products, but quality of the environment'. It is time we all emulated his example, and began to look beyond the end of our own noses.

I welcome this book. It is proof that organic wine is at last being taken seriously. People have finally got the message that organic wine is not made from rhubarb. It cannot be said often enough that chemicals, except in small doses, are not necessary for the production of good wine. There is poor non-organic wine, just as there is poor organic wine. Judge the producers listed here on their own merits — as winemakers, not as cranks. Most of them deserve your attention and support.

INTRODUCTION

ORGANIC WINES

Organic wines are different from ordinary wines. They are made from organically grown grapes; the grapes come from vines cultivated without the use of synthetic chemical fertilizers, or pesticides. Permitted additives are few, and those actually used are fewer still. Most organic producers join an independent organic association which acts as both a control and a support. These bodies have regulations that must be followed in order to conform with organic winemaking practices. Wine growers are then allowed to display the symbol of the organic association they belong to on their wine label. This logo indicates that the wine has been made organically according to a certain standard. In voluntarily and publicly declaring their method of cultivation, the organic producers are one step ahead of the secretive conventional winemakers, commonly known in France as the *chimi*.

In addition to the possible danger to consumers, *chimi* wine production contributes to the destruction of the environment. Eco-systems are disturbed, the soil is broken down and the vines become hooked into the cycle of chemical feeds and treatments. Organically made wines, like all organic products, are the result of an approach which aims to work with, rather than against, the delicate balance of nature. As part of this overall approach the producers are likely to take on board other compatible philosophies which, while not being specific to organic methods, logically complement them — for example, the concepts of quality rather than quantity; individuality of style rather than bland uniformity; or the combination of the best traditional methods with the benefits of modern technology.

Late in the summer of 1990, the wine trade was thrown into

turmoil. Thousands of cases of wine from France, Spain and Italy imported into the USA were impounded by customs officials because of fears that they contained traces of an illegal pesticide. The ban was imposed following tests on three consignments of wine that had revealed residues of the Japanese-produced fungicide *procymidone*. Though this chemical is used by wine producers the world over, its use is forbidden in the USA where no products can be sold that contain even minute amounts. European wine producers faced the choice of having to switch to an entirely different fungicide that did conform to American standards, or risk losing the market.

This raises the obvious question for the consumer — how often do we run the risk of inadvertently drinking fungicide residues when we open a bottle of wine? Nor does the risk stop at fungicides. There is a whole host of synthetic chemical fertilizers and pesticides which are used in the vineyard — herbicides, insecticides, fungicides. Where do they go? Do they end up in the wine? Is there a 'safe' amount to consume? And what about the additives that are introduced after the grapes have been picked, whilst the wine is being made?

The place to find answers to these questions should be the label on the wine bottle. But information on wine labels is only about the type of wine — details of country, region, vintage, grape variety and so on. There is nothing to tell us what the liquid in the bottle actually contains. We could expect additives, and any pesticide residues. In fact there is total secrecy. Astonishingly, it is not obligatory for producers or for retailers of wine in the UK to ensure that ingredients are printed on the label. This is utterly without justification. Food and non-alcoholic drinks, like orange squash, must list this information, in the form of E numbers, or the chemicals described in terms of their function, or merely their chemical names. For example, sulphur dioxide may be listed as 'E220' or as 'preservative', or as 'sulphur dioxide'. But neither ingredients nor additives need be declared at all on alcoholic drinks — except the low-alcohol variety (less than 1.2 per cent alcohol by volume) when, illogically, such listing is obligatory.

If the same rules were applied to wine, we would be told about the chemicals that were consciously added, such as sulphur dioxide, tartaric acid or ascorbic acid. But this would still not include the residual presence of chemicals which were applied during the cultivation of the grapes. We ought to be told if these chemicals are there so that we can decide whether their presence bothers us or not.

ADDITIVES – EXCEEDING THE LIMITS

An astonishing number of chemicals are permitted in the production of wine (see page 25). The rules as to how such chemicals can be used, and in what quantities, are clearly laid down by the authorities governing wine production in each country. However, the rules can be broken and indeed *are* broken in a whole number of ways, some more dangerous to the consumer's health than others.

Quite a number of cases revolve around the use of legally permitted additives used in illegally excessive quantities.

Sorbitol is a naturally occurring sweetener. It was found to have been used in excess of permitted levels in several of the leading brands of Chilean wines in 1990, and also in some wines from the Australian Tyrell company in 1988. It is contained in several fruits, including grapes, and is approved as an additive for foods including ice cream and chewing gum. As far as is known, it does not do any harm, but because the wine companies concerned had exceeded the specified limits, they were breaking the rules. In this case, the rules were not to protect human safety, but to guarantee authenticity and quality.

Probably the most frequent example of 'fraud' involves chaptalization of wine. This is when sugar is added to the must, or unfermented juice, prior to fermentation in order to raise the alcohol level. It is illegal in some countries, like Italy, but allowed in others, like France, in certain regions. It is known to take place more frequently than is officially recognized.

In 1989 the very reputable Burgundy firm of 'Bouchard Père et Fils' was taken to court for over-chaptalizing its wines, and for adding tartaric acid. They had committed these felonies because the vintage in question, 1987, had produced juice of inferior quality, lacking in sufficient natural sugar to produce the required alcohol level. It also lacked sufficient acidity to give the wine bite and balance, so the extra tartaric acid was introduced. Such practices are by no means the preserve of this particular company. They are well-known throughout Burgundy and elsewhere.

The rules had been broken, but there was no suggestion of the action posing a danger to human health. The issue at stake here is one of misrepresentation or cheating. In both these cases extra additives were used to make a so-called 'better' wine. In terms of the usual criteria for judging the quality of a wine, the extra additives simply improved the finished product. The producers cheated and the public were misled about what they were buying. There were plenty of voices at the time screaming 'so what?'. If the additives are not dangerous and the wine improved, why not use them?

An entirely different form of deception took place in the now infamous case of the so-called 'antifreeze scandal'. In Austria in 1985, a VAT inspector carrying out a routine inspection uncovered massive purchases of diethylene glycol by a wine merchant. It transpired that the chemical was being used on a very large scale as an additive to wines because it gave added 'body' and sweetness, so improving what were otherwise inferior wines.

The use of diethylene glycol was a clever move by the winemaker responsible because it was not a substance that the authorities would normally look for in wine. It was almost certainly in use for many years before its discovery. The thoroughness and efficiency of the authorities in analysing wines is a major cause for concern. The presence of residues left by permitted chemicals can be tested for, time and resources allowing. The frequency of routine sample testing can never be too great. But the likelihood of detecting a chemical which is not normally used in wine production is slim. The scope for using illegal and possibly dangerous additives in winemaking is worrying, to say the least. In the famous Italian scandal an unspecified number of people died after drinking cheap wine tainted with methanol.

PESTICIDES — CAN YOU TRUST THEM?

The procymidone scare (page 10) aptly encapsulates the problem of pesticide contamination. Here was a product that had satisfied the safety testing procedures of most countries and had been declared safe to use yet had been banned in the USA. The actual amount of chemical detected was tiny, and well within the recommended limit set by the World Health Organization. Surely, then, there should have been no risk to health?

The safety of pesticides is a hotly debated issue. On the one hand the manufacturers point out that their products have to go through the most stringent safety tests before they can be approved for sale. Where residues occur in wine they are usually in infinitesimally small amounts — equivalent to a grain of salt in a swimming pool. Set against this is the fact that many chemicals in use in wine production are known to produce cancer and birth defects in laboratory test animals. According to the London Food Commission, for example, insecticides sprayed in vineyards could contain up to 49 substances that might cause cancer, and 61 that could lead to birth defects. A report by the National Research Council in the United States, concerned with pesticide use in agriculture in general, found that 30 per cent of insecticides, 60 per cent of herbicides and 90 per cent of fungicides were capable of producing tumours if used in excess.

However stringent and thorough laboratory tests might be, they can only give an indication of how a pesticide might behave once it is in general use. It is usually after a substance has been used for a number of years that unexpected side-effects are noticed, at which point the pesticide is withdrawn from sale. Unfortunately, different countries operate different criteria when judging whether or not to allow certain chemicals. The herbicide 245T, for example, better known as the chemical warfare weapon Agent Orange used in Vietnam, has long been banned in the USA, Germany and all Scandinavian countries, but may still be legally sold in Britain. Paraquat, a best-selling herbicide, is allowed in the UK but banned in the Netherlands. As more of the older pesticides, which were cleared for sale at a time when testing was more lax, come up for review, the list of banned substances is likely to grow. Table 1 lists those that have been banned in the UK since 1984.

In all of this, what is unclear is the long-term threat to health posed by continual exposure to low levels of pesticide residues acting either alone or in combination with other food additives. It is extremely difficult to carry out laboratory experiments that might predict the outcome, or to diagnose whether responsibility for a particular disease can be laid at the door of pesticide contamination. For these reasons it is unlikely that the issue of pesticide safety will be resolved in the near future. In the meantime, for those who don't wish to take the risk, the answer is to buy organic.

Many people are surprised at the wide range of organic wines on offer. Contrary to general expectations, they are not made from pea pods or organic lentils, or even old socks! Most have a freshness and individuality that is sadly lacking in so many mass-produced conventional wines. Some of the better organic wines are absolutely outstanding — particularly those which might otherwise suffer from being over-sulphured. As regards sulphur, it is said that because of the absence of additives you get less of a hangover from organic wine. For this reason, but not this reason alone, we commend it to you. Bonne santé!

TABLE 1:
PESTICIDES BANNED IN THE UK SINCE 1984

Pesticide	Use	Suspected Risk	Date banned
Aldrin	Insecticide	Carcinogen/ Teratogen/ Mutagen	1989
Binapacryl	Fungicide	Teratogen	1987
Bitertanol	Fungicide	Teratogen	1985
Captafol	Fungicide	Carcinogen/ Teratogen/ Mutagen	1989
Cyhexatin	Acaracide (kills mites)	Teratogen	1988
DDT	Insecticide	Carcinogen/ Teratogen/ Mutagen	1964-84
Dieldrin	Insecticide	Carcinogen/ Teratogen/ Mutagen	1989
Dinoseb	Herbicide	Teratogen	1988
DNOC	Insecticide	Teratogen	1989
Ethylene dibromide	Fumigant	Carcinogen	1985
Endrin	Insecticide	Carcinogen/ Teratogen/ Mutagen	1964-84
Chlordane	Earthworm killer	Carcinogen/ Teratogen/ Mutagen	1992

Notes:
carcinogen: may cause or promote cancer
teratogen: may cause reproductive problems, e.g. deformed offspring
mutagen: may damage genes and chromosomes; possible abnormalities in future
generations.

HOW TO USE
THIS BOOK

This book is divided into two distinct parts. Part One describes how organic wine is made, and what sets it apart from conventional production, from the cultivation of the grapes through to the manufacture of the wine. An important factor, from the consumer point of view, is the verification procedure. How can you be sure that organic wine is what it claims to be? What do the organic quality marks look like and what else should you look out for on the wine label? Finally, the section ends with a chapter on serving, storing and tasting wine.

Part Two describes some 500 wines from all over the world that are currently on sale in the UK. Each is described in turn, giving basic information including vintage, whether suitable for vegetarians or vegans, and a guide to the qualities of the wine. Most of the wines are available by mail order direct from the importers, and a small but increasing number are on sale in the high street — either in supermarkets or through retail chains. A number of wholefood shops, quality delicatessens and specialist wine shops are now selling organic wines, and a selected list of some of those stocking a comprehensive range can be found in Chapter 8. For the independent stockist near you, consult the specialist importers and wholesalers. (Chapter 9).

PART ONE

1

GROWING THE GRAPES

The character of a particular wine — and this means the overall impression given by what it looks, smells and tastes like — is a result of what happens when the grapes are growing in the vineyard and when they are processed. Getting it right at both stages is crucial to the final quality of the wine. If the grapes are poor, the wine can never be more than mediocre in quality. On the other hand, the very best grapes can be turned into poor wine by an inadequate winemaker. High quality grapes together with high quality winemaking produce high quality wine, whether organic or otherwise. Organically grown grapes should provide the best basis from which to make quality wine.

Organic wine, put at its simplest, is wine made from grapes that have been grown without the use of any synthetic fertilizers or pesticides. This does not mean that organic growers manage their vineyards without using fertilizers or sprays at all. Natural fertilizers, compost and manures are necessary for maintaining and improving soil fertility in an organic vineyard and, though sprays are actively discouraged, there is a range of non-synthetic pesticides available to combat attack from pests and diseases. To a large extent, the chief difference between a conventional and an organic grower depends on their overall approach to growing rather than the products they use in the vineyard.

Organic agriculture is based on working *with* rather than *against* nature. It is a system which positively seeks to regenerate the soil as a source of sustenance for the crops. Instead of waging chemical warfare on the land (only to have to add more chemicals to make amends), organic methods actively encourage a natural equilibrium. Enriching the life of the soil leads to stronger, healthier crops, more resistant to disease and pests than their chemically dependent cousins. Prevention rather than cure is the philosophy wherever possible. Organic quality is concerned with purity, safety, health and internal characteristics of the product rather than its external appearance.

One thing that organic does not mean is old-fashioned and cranky. On the contrary: an organic approach learns from the past, incorporating the best traditional methods with more recent scientific advances. Organic methods safeguard the long-term well-being of both the environment and the consumer.

GETTING DOWN TO BASICS — THE SOIL

Organic wine begins with the microbes in the soil which nourish the plant. In conventional vine growing, the soil is often dead. Chemicals used to kill weeds, insects and fungi can also destroy the beneficial microbes and bacteria that work in the living soil and release nutrients. The vines are not adequately nourished, so they need chemical fertilizers. These are soluble salts which do not enrich the soil, but act as a direct feed to the plant. The vines, therefore, come to live in the soil, but not of it. The roots of a vine would normally search down far into the ground, drawing on nutrients. With chemical fertilizers the roots rest near the surface, waiting for their next fix. Not being integrated with a living soil, the vines do not develop their own internal strength and resistance. This in turn means that fungal diseases and insect pests provide a greater danger. Lacking adequate defences of their own, the vines are treated with chemical fungicides and insecticides. This further reinforces the cycle of dependence on external chemical aids.

In an organic vineyard the aim is to produce strong, healthy vines that bear pure, top-quality fruit. In place of dependence on the chemical cycle, the vine's own resources are built up, giving the plant greater strength. The soil is enriched with organic compost and fertilizers, made from a variety of materials. These include animal manures; waste products from the fermentation of the wine including yeast deposits; sediments left after clarification and the 'marc' (pressed skins and stalks); vine leaves; prunings and straw. Usually these are composted before being spread on the ground under the vines as a 'mulch'. Gradually the material is incorporated into the soil through the action of earthworms and other soil-living creatures. Here it is further broken down by countless micro-organisms — as many as five billion to a teaspoon of soil — into the basic plant nutrients that are then taken up by the vines.

It is important, though, that soil analyses are taken from time to time, to ensure that the soil acidity is kept at the right level and to prevent the development of nutrient shortages.

If this happens, natural minerals can be added in controlled amounts by the application of such treatments as powdered rocks and bone, phosphates, and seaweed.

GRAPE TYPES

One of the big unanswered questions in vine growing, organic or not, is 'Which is more important, the grape or the soil?'. Opinions differ among wine experts, with some, such as Jancis Robinson, suggesting that the grape is responsible for as much as 90 per cent of the character of a wine.

Though there are in excess of 1000 different grape varieties available for the production of wine, only a small proportion of these are used in the wines that we drink.

Which are the best, or greatest, grape varieties is something of a personal opinion, though the red wine grapes Cabernet Sauvignon, Pinot Noir, Syrah and Merlot, and the white wine grapes Riesling, Chardonnay, Semillon, Sauvignon and Chenin Blanc, would probably figure in most wine connoisseurs' lists. Hard on their heels might come Gamay, Sangiovese, Zinfandel, Granache, Tempranillo and Carignan for the reds, and Gewürztraminer, Muscat, Muscadet, Müller-Thurgau and Silvaner for the whites. These vines produce both the best and some of the most popular wines in the world.

All wine-producing regions have their own local, traditional variety of vine. But increasingly vines are quite literally travelling the planet, as producers seek to plant a variety that is both popular and marketable as well as being suited to their particular local conditions. The grape variety itself now often appears on the wine label and, particularly in the case of the Chardonnay grape, is in danger of becoming a generic term in its own right much as 'Hoover' is.

Chardonnay is now one of the most internationally popular grape types wherever it is grown. It produces some of the best dry white wines available. Growers all over the world have recognized its power in the market. In Burgundy, where much of the white wine has for years been made from Chardonnay, the name of this prestigious region used to be sufficient to sell the wine. Nowadays many Burgundians tacitly accept that the grape name rivals the region in selling power and have added it to their labels. 'I like Chardonnay' might seem a baffling comment in view of the enormous differences in style that this grape can produce — from the very full-flavoured Australian Chardonnays to the light, fruity, delicate wine produced in parts of southern France. The fact that people say they like Chardonnay across the board can be put down to good marketing.

Despite the popularity of certain varieties, it is important for growers to match the vine and the soil accurately to achieve optimum results. Vines tend to thrive on what would traditionally be considered poor agricultural land. It seems that the harder the struggle, the better, as far as the plant is concerned.

Good combinations of soil and grape are those such as Cabernet Sauvignon (the great red grape of the Medoc on Bordeaux's western seaboard, and home of the world's greatest wines) with gravel which gives good drainage. Chardonnay and Sauvignon grow well on chalk and limestone soils. Riesling thrives on slate. However, the recent great successes in Australia and the USA have been achieved by using these grape varieties on totally different soils. As a result, the conventional wisdom is being challenged.

WINE GROWING REGIONS

Grapes are grown in some pretty unlikely regions, but the main commercial areas all fall within the 30—50 degrees latitude bands, north and south of the equator. If you look at a world map (see Figure 1) you can identify the major wine-producing regions running across the globe within this band, from California in the west to Australia in the east. They cannot grow vines in Iceland, and it is hard enough in Somerset, so it's not difficult to appreciate the importance of the climate in wine production.

Essentially, vines and grapes need water, heat and light. Too little of any of these, or too much, at the wrong time in the growing season, creates problems. In cold climates, such as Germany or England, the lack of heat and light means that grapes may not ripen properly and the sugar content of the grape may therefore be low. In hot climates, such as north Africa, the sun can burn the leaves and tremendous heat requires irrigation to provide sufficient water. As a generalization, hot climate wines tend to be heavier in alcohol, since well-ripened grapes produce more natural sugar which

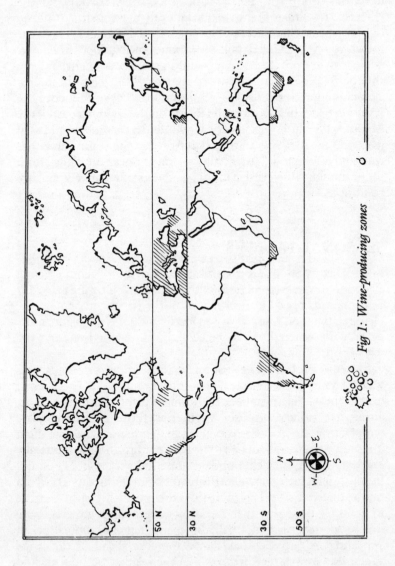

Fig 1: Wine-producing zones

ferments to make more alcohol. They also produce more immediate, strong up-front flavours. Cold climate wines will be lower in alcohol, with more subtle, less obvious flavours.

The micro-climate of the vineyard site can be crucial in getting the right combination of factors to grow good quality grapes. This is the reason you hear so much talk about south-facing slopes in France. Vines grown on hillsides facing south get more sunlight, and are thus better positioned. The micro-climate is like a jigsaw of specific factors unique to each site — all fitting together to influence the resulting wine. In Bordeaux the forests on the western coast of the Medoc act as a buffer against the sea winds. In Provence the Mistral (the cold northerly wind that sweeps across the plain) can either ruin the harvest or act beneficially by cleaning away any danger from rot or mould, which thrive in still, humid or alternatively very dry conditions.

SEASONAL FACTORS

Like other types of crop cultivation, viticulture requires close attention to the seasonal cycle of the plant. The growing season in Europe is mainly from February until the harvest in September/October. The soil must have adequate nutrients, the plants must be properly watered, weeds prevented from taking over, and the temperature controlled.

To ensure protection against night frosts, growers in the Rhône valley have introduced large stones into the vineyard. These retain heat in the day, giving it back to the fragile plants during the night, rather like storage heaters. Another method used to regulate temperature is to place thermometers in the vineyard and wire them up to trigger off an alarm bell if the temperature drops to a critically low level. When the bell sounds all and sundry leap out of bed and furiously light fires to increase the temperature. Sometimes the cold can be disastrous. In France in 1990 the unusually warm weather in early spring meant that the plants began their growing cycle much sooner than normal. In many regions shoots began appearing in early February, 4 to 6 weeks ahead of the usual timescale. Growers were worried that the weather would turn cold again, and that frosts would kill the budding plants. This is exactly what happened in parts of the Loire valley. One small family estate, making excellent Muscadet de Sèvre et Maine, lost about 75 per cent of its potential crop, a disaster for any producer. Others in the region also lost significant amounts. The location of the vineyard determined how different growers fared. This of course drives up prices, as supply becomes severely restricted.

Just as dangerous as the frost is hail. In early June 1990, a producer in the south of France, near Beziers, showed photographs of his vines, before and after a hailstorm. The first picture showed vibrant, healthy plants with nicely growing foliage; the second depicted torn and wasted leaves hanging scraggily off the battered plants. He too will have very little to sell during 1991.

GROWING PROBLEMS

It is in the control of pests and diseases that organic growers depart most noticeably from their chemical-using equivalents.

Vines, like any other plant, are liable to attack from a variety of organisms. A conventional grower responds to this threat by using synthetic pesticides and there is now a huge arsenal of chemicals from which to choose.

TABLE 2: PERMITTED SYNTHETIC CHEMICALS USED ON VINES IN BRITAIN

Diseases	Botrytis Downy mildew Powdery mildew	Chlorothalonil, dichlofluanid vinclozolin, metalaxyl, cufraneb, mancozeb, triadimefon, copper oxychloride, fenarimol.
Pests	Aphids Capsids Mealy bugs Red spider mites Scale insects Thrips	Cypermethrin, dimethoate, petroleum, oil, tetradifon.
Weeds	—	Diquat, paraquat, propyzamide simazine, glyphosate, oxadiazon.

NB: a far greater list of chemicals is approved for use on the Continent.

Fungal diseases are the biggest problem and many conventional producers adopt a programme of so-called insurance spraying of the vines with fungicides, every fortnight from spring to harvest. It is not difficult to see how under such circumstances grapes may be produced which contain unacceptably high levels of pesticides.

This is compounded by the fact that pests and diseases tend to build up an immunity to the chemicals that are used against them. Continual use of the same pesticide encourages resistant strains to develop as the susceptible individuals are weeded out. The temptation is to use the chemical in ever-stronger doses to get the same effect. In the end this is self-defeating and this particular pesticide, no longer able to exert any control on the pest at all, is discarded in favour of a different one. The process whereby pests and diseases become resistant to pesticides is now happening at an accelerating rate, causing great anxiety in the minds of growers as to whether new pesticides can be developed fast enough.

THE ORGANIC WAY

By contrast, the primary method of dealing with problems in an organic vineyard is natural prevention rather than cure. Strong organically-cultivated vines are able to withstand attack better than their 'chimi' counterparts. Some of the worst fungal diseases, such as Botrytis (grey rot) are much more frequent where nitrogen-rich chemical fertilizers have been used.

The incidence of problems with pests and diseases varies regionally in accordance with the climate. It is easier to make organic wine in Provence, in the relatively disease-free south of France, than in the colder climates of Burgundy or the Loire. Damp and humid climates can encourage fungal growth. This difference notwithstanding, it is very common for an organic grower who practises preventative techniques, to answer the question 'What do you do about all these pests if you cannot use pesticides?' by replying 'Pests, what pests?'. With the notable exception of mildew, our experience is that most organic wine producers do not suffer from pests or diseases to a commercially prohibitive extent.

As well as relying on the inherent health and vigour that comes with organic techniques, the vigneron depends to a major extent, particularly in the control of insect pests, on the pests' natural enemies.

Interplanting

One of the ways of encouraging greater numbers of natural foes lies in a technique known as interplanting. It is one of the more attractive sights in an organic vineyard, with plants such as flowers, herbs and legumes growing in between the rows of vines. Specific types of plants are chosen to attract birds, mammals and insects which act as predators on the pests which threaten the vine. For example, ladybirds and hoverflies appear and eat the greenfly. Parasitic wasps are lured to the area and then go on to lay their eggs in the bodies of insect pests nearby. Other plants are chosen to act as decoys so that pests are encouraged to attack them rather than the vines.

Leguminous plants such as clovers have bacteria living on their roots that 'fix' nitrogen from the atmosphere. If these clover plants are subsequently ploughed in they decay, releasing the nitrogen into the soil where it can be taken up by the vine as a natural fertilizer. It is even possible to combine the sorts of plants described above with commercial crops such as strawberries, which when grown between the rows add to the economic viability of the exercise. The final effect of interplanting is that, by reducing monoculture, a more balanced environment is created which provides a general lessening of the risk of serious attack from pests and diseases.

This is not to say that organic growers do entirely without pesticides. Rot and mould are probably the biggest problems of all in the organic vineyard. The traditional preventative measures (there are no effective cures) are to spray the vines with 'Bordeaux mixture' (lime and copper sulphate) and sulphur. These naturally derived substances are both permitted in organic and in 'chimi' production — although the frequency of spraying is greatly reduced for an organic grower. While it is common to spray 14 or 15 times a year in conventional vineyards, organic growers spray as infrequently as possible — depending on the climate, perhaps as little as 2 or 3 times a year. Restrictions are placed on spraying near harvest time, to avoid the chemical contamination of the fermenting juice and subsequently the wine that we drink. Bordeaux mixture and sulphur are both used as 'contact' sprays. This means that when sprayed on they remain on the leaves of the plant. This is in direct contrast to many synthetic fungicides which are often 'systemic', meaning that they are taken into the internal system of the plant where they remain effective for a longer period than that achieved by contact sprays. They are carried to all parts of the vine, including the grape. The danger is, of course, that they are more likely to be present in the finished wine.

If beneficial insects and other natural enemies do not appear to be keeping pests under control, the organic grower has a number of further options. Plant, herbal or mineral-based sprays exist and more are being developed and approved. Two plant-based insecticides — pyrethrum, derived from chrysanthemums, and rotenone, from a tropical plant called Derris — are frequently permitted in organic systems. These are effective against aphids and the 'ver de la grappe' or caterpillars. Both insecticides have a make-up which allows them to break down rapidly. This enables them to be used against specific targets without lingering to affect others.

Biological Control

A second method is 'biological control'. This involves importing a natural enemy of the pest which then controls it through predation or parasitism. For example, the red spider mite, which does an enormous amount of damage to vine leaves, can be kept in check by a predatory red spider mite called *Phytoseiuilus persimilis*. Specific caterpillar pests are controlled by use of a bacterial insecticide called *Bacillus thuringiensis*. This naturally-occurring bacterium is sprayed onto the vine leaves. When eaten it reacts in the highly alkaline conditions present in the caterpillar's gut causing paralysis and death. To all other species it is entirely harmless.

Insect Traps

Bright yellow painted sticky traps hanging amongst the grapes attract many pests, and special lures of a sexual kind have been developed. These pheromone traps, as they are known, contain synthetic extracts of the chemical scents that many insects put out when attracting mates. As with the bacterial insecticides they are highly specific in nature and result in a collection of unfortunate male insects which have been lured to a sticky end. Research into providing new organic ways of dealing with insect pests continues all the time and is infinitely preferable to the use of chemicals which, all too often, are found to be dangerous to bees, wild birds, animals and perhaps people.

WEEDS

If not checked, weeds can compete with vines for nutrients and water. During the last twenty years weedkillers, or herbicides, have been used increasingly to keep down weeds by conventional growing. We are now beginning to see the effects of such practices, in the sinister increase of herbicidal residues found in drinking water. So persistent can some of these chemicals be, that soil can be poisoned to a depth of several feet, threatening the health of the vine itself. This is particularly so after dry seasons where large quantities of chemical get flushed all at once to the rooting area.

In her book *Vine Growing in Britain,* Gillian Pearkes tells of a forest in south Wales that has been kept clear of weeds by using herbicides for many years. The poison build-up is now so great that the ground is in fact dead. All attempts to replant this area with young trees fail year after year.

There are no organic weedkillers. Once again organic growers rely on a combination of methods to keep weeds under control. These can include weeding by hand or machine or the use of mulches to smother out weeds. The aim is not to wipe out weeds completely — after all they are used to make compost — but to ensure that they do not adversely compete with the vines.

WHO ARE THE ORGANIC WINEMAKERS?

Organic wine still represents a tiny proportion of total wine production — probably a fraction of 1 per cent. Of all wine-producing countries, France produces the largest number of bottles of organic wine and also has the greatest number of growers. There are no easily identifiable statistics for either of these. The 'independent' organic producers who do not belong to an official organic association make numbers even more difficult to ascertain. On a count of commercially active 'verified' producers only, we would estimate the approximate numbers to be 200 in France, 130 in Germany, 40 in Italy, 2 in Spain, 1 in Portugal, 1 in New Zealand, 1 in Australia, 3 in California, 1 in Hungary and 2 in England. The number of independent organic producers is not known.

The organic winemakers are a diverse collection of people. In France and Italy, two particular strands stand out, the traditionalists and the *jeunes*. The traditionalists are those whose families have been making wine using natural methods for generations. The 'jeunes' are those who have been converted by more recent political and environmental concerns. Some are 'returnees', the post-1968 generation who have gone back to the land to work in a more natural environment. Others have taken over the family property from their parents and converted it to organic methods. Several have abandoned chemicals after becoming ill due to accidents including inhalation of the sprays. Others simply regard it as part and parcel of making a good wine. Only once have we come across a producer who has openly stated his motive as financial — rightly believing that there would be a burgeoning market for organic wines in the future. No doubt more will be tempted down this path.

Today's organic wine producer is typically a small, quality-conscious family concern, sometimes growing a few other complementary crops. It is unlikely that the economics of the wine trade will see this change radically in the near future. The day when the giants of the drinks industry go organic is still some way off.

2

MAKING THE WINE

The essential elements of turning grapes into wine are quite straightforward. Once the grapes have been picked they are usually pressed to extract the juice, which is then put in a clean vat for fermentation. Fermentation takes from a few days to several weeks. The newly-made wine may then be filtered and bottled more or less straight away, but is more usually stored — for anything from a few months to several years, depending on the style.

This simplified description conceals what today can be a very complex affair. Much conventional wine production is the result of a highly technological processing operation — one that may also involve the use of an array of different additives. It is in the extent of this processing and the use of such additives that the organic winemaker differs from his conventional neighbour.

YEASTS

Wine is made by the action of yeasts on the natural sugars found in grape juice, which are fermented into alcohol and carbon dioxide. Yeasts are present naturally on the skins of grapes and once the skin has been broken and the juice released, fermentation will begin.

On chemically grown grapes, however, there are not too many natural yeasts left, as most will have been destroyed by repeated fungicidal sprays. Under such circumstances, cultured yeasts may have to be introduced by conventional vignerons to start off fermentation. Even if the natural yeasts have survived, they are often deliberately killed off with a dose of sulphur dioxide so that a standard cultured yeast can be introduced. This particularly applies where standardization of the wine style is all-important, as in the production of high-volume processed wines such as Liebfraumilch. As part of a commitment to individuality and the natural process, organic growers normally ferment using the natural yeast found on the grape skins.

ALCOHOL LEVELS

Whichever type of yeast is selected, if left to itself it will go on working until all the sugar has been converted into alcohol, thus producing a dry wine. However, wine yeasts die naturally when the alcohol level reaches around 15 per cent, and if there is sufficient sugar in the juice initially it is possible to end up with a sweet wine containing 15 per cent alcohol.

In fact the amount of sugar in the finished wine varies enormously according to grape type, different regions and countries, and within the same region, from one year to the next. A typical French red from Bordeaux will end up at around 12 per cent alcohol. From the Rhône valley, where it is generally hotter, it is more likely to be around 13.5 per cent. Similarly in Australia or north Africa, the hot climate leads to pretty high-alcohol wines, around 13–14 per cent. In colder Germany on the other hand, wines of only 8 or 9 per cent are common.

In some countries, in regions where a specific degree of alcohol is essential for the balance and quality of the wine, additional sugar may be added to the grape juice before fermentation. This is only done with permission from the regulating body. The wine is not sweeter as a result, because the extra sugar is all turned into alcohol. This process is known as *chaptalization* after the Frenchman, Jean-Antoine Chaptal (Napoleon's Minister of Agriculture) who came up with the idea. It is a common practice in Beaujolais and Alsace, but it is not allowed in Italy, for example.

STORAGE

Nowadays fermentation is usually carried out in stainless steel vats. Most wines will then be stored for a short time before bottling — most commonly in vats made of cement, steel or wood. Both white and red types of wine may be stored in small oak barrels to give added flavour to the wines, although the practice is more commonly used for reds.

For white wines the aim is usually to preserve the flavour of the fresh fruit. There has however been a lot of experimentation with storing white wines, particularly Chardonnay and Sauvignon, in oak barrels over the past few years. The flavour is affected by the age of the barrel, its size, and what kind of wood it is made from; also on the wine's length of stay. If the barrel is new, small, made from French Limousin oak, and the wine is stored in it for 6—9 months there will be a very strong flavour from the barrel in the taste of the wine.

This was common in many Australian dry white wines until recently; some people love the woody flavour, others think that the flavour of the fruit is overpowered, and cynics say it can be a good way of disguising a poor wine!

If a red wine is stored in very large old oak vats that hold thousands of litres, the flavour of the wine will probably not be altered much, if at all. When stored in small new oak vats, much added character will be given to the wine, complementing the tannins already present. At the end of the day, oak or not, it all boils down to personal preference.

CLARIFYING THE WINE

Nobody wants to drink a wine that is full of little bits of debris. Commercially-produced wines are therefore clear, and bright. Clarifying the wine can be achieved by fining, filtering, centrifuging or simply by the action of time. If a wine is left undisturbed in a cold cellar for long enough it will settle and clear naturally. Daniel Combe at Vignoble de la Jasse in the Rhône is one of several organic winemakers who adopt this approach. His wine is neither fined nor filtered. But others need to speed up the process to get their wine into the shops as soon as possible.

FINING

A fining agent is a substance which is added to a vat of wine to clear it of particles. It works by gradually sinking from top to bottom, collecting floating solids on the way down.

The most common fining agents in organic production are egg whites, and bentonite or keiselghur clays. Also permitted by several organizations, but less often used, are pure casein (a milk derivative), isinglass (made from the swim bladder of a sturgeon fish), and food quality natural gelatine (from bones).

TABLE 3: ADDITIVES COMMONLY USED IN THE CLARIFICATION AND FINING OF WINES

Product	'E' number	Comment	Organic viewpoint
Edible gelatine		Can be made from bones or vegetable base	Permitted only if not hydrolysed
Isinglass		A coagulant made from the swim bladder of the sturgeon fish. Produces brilliance in a wine	Permitted
Casein and Potassium caseinate		Derived from milk. Possible allergenic	Permitted in its pure form guaranteed free of residues; forbidden as industrial casein
Animal albumen		Egg white	Permitted and recommended
Bentonite	558	A clay. Kieselguhr is another similar product	Permitted
Silicon dioxide as gel or colloidal solution	551	Also acts as a stabilizer. A rock-forming mineral	Permitted
Kaolin	559	A mineral made from granite	Permitted but not recommended
Potassium ferrocyanide (Blue finings)	536	Used to remove excess iron or copper from wines. Ferrocyanides are recognised as potential anaemia forming substances. They are banned in Germany and the USA but allowed by EC	Forbidden
Tannin		Used to remove gelatin	Forbidden

Product	'E' number	Comment	Organic viewpoint
Metatartaric acid	E353	Used to remove excess calcium in wines. Derived from tartaric acid	Forbidden
Pectinolytic enzymes	E440(a)		Forbidden
Enzymatic preparation of betaglucanase		Prevents haze formation	Forbidden

Other: Blood, alginates and industrial casein are also sometimes used in commercial wine production but are prohibited by Nature et Progrès.

Whilst most of these substances appear to be safe, there are question marks over some of them. Potassium ferrocyanide, for example, is a by-product of coal gas manufacture and is banned in Germany and the USA.

Various types of acid, in particular tartaric acid, which are present in the wine crystallize in cold temperatures and drop to the bottom of the vat. The wine can then be siphoned off, leaving the crystals behind. Wines that have not had the tartrate crystals precipitated out may well produce them at a later date, often once they are on sale in the shops. The crystals are harmless, but as they do not look attractive and retailers want to avoid a stream of complaining customers returning bottles to their stores, the wines containing crystals are usually sold at a fraction of their proper price. Buy them when you can, especially if the wine on offer is something a bit special that you would not normally be able to afford or be likely to try. You simply have to pour the wine out carefully, or decant it into another bottle, leaving the crystals behind. Then make the most of your bargain!

FILTRATION

Before bottling, the wines will usually be filtered through cellulose sheets to complete the clarifying process. Until relatively recently, asbestos was used as a filtering agent, but this is now banned. Filtering not only removes unwanted particles but also some of the enzymes that give the wine its flavour, and so some of the best organic wines are made without fining or filtering. They are simply left in a cool cellar for the bits and pieces to settle, producing a beautifully clear wine. Again it is often the commercial need to speed things up that necessitates introducing greater inputs into the process.

Filtering is usually necessary for white wines that are being sold in the year after they are harvested. Reds are stored for several years before being sold and thus have more time to clear naturally.

PRESERVATION AND STERILIZATION

Sulphur is the principal additive in wine. Its role is to sterilize and preserve. It helps to prevent oxidation and may be added to wines at various stages of the winemaking process. When the 'must' is starting to ferment, sulphur may be added to kill the yeasts, or to 'fix' the wine. It can be added later to stop fermentation, and again before bottling to act as a preservative. Sulphur is also used to sterilize equipment. Sulphur dioxide (also known by its chemical name, SO_2, or its E number E220) causes headaches, stomach aches, hangovers and sometimes acute reactions in asthma sufferers. It destroys Vitamin B_1. Without question, the lower the sulphur level in a wine, the better for health. By and large it is the cheaper end of the wine market that suffers most from the over-use of sulphur. Essentially sulphur is a cheap alternative to tender loving care in winemaking, overcoming problems of poor quality control and less than perfect hygiene.

This having been said, sulphur dioxide is permitted in the production of organic wines in very restricted amounts. A few organic winemakers add no sulphur at all and several add very little. The maximum amounts allowed vary from country to country, region to region, and from one type of wine to another. Sweet wines always contain higher sulphur levels than dry, and red wines generally have less sulphur than whites. There are two ways of measuring sulphur in a wine — the 'total' and 'free' contents. Total refers to the amount added initially, free to the amount that remains eventually. The reason for the difference is that sulphur dioxide interacts with other chemicals in the wine in such a way that it is reduced in concentration with time. Tiny amounts of sulphur may be present in finished wine even when none has been added, because sulphur can occur naturally as a by-product of fermentation.

Many organic wine producers in fact use far less sulphur than the maximum permitted under organic regulations. Analysis of the 1989 red wine of the Cave Co-operative at Villelieu in the Rhône valley showed only 18 milligrams per litre had been added against a permitted 60; only traces were present in the residual free analysis, against a permitted 10 mg/l.

TABLE 4: MAXIMUM PERMITTED LEVELS OF SULPHUR DIOXIDE (SO_2) IN FRENCH WINE (MG/L)[1]

Region	Red Wines			White Wines		
	EC	Nature et Progrès		EC	Nature et Progrès	
	Total	Total	Free	Total	Total	Free
Bordeaux and Bergerac	210(SW) 160(D)	90	20	400*(SW) 210(D)	240 (SW) 100(D)	60(SW) 30(D)
Beaujolais	210(SW) 160(D)	50	10	210(D)	70	20
Champagne	210(SW) 160(D)	—	—	185**(SP)	60(SP)	12(SP)
Alsace	210(SW) 160(D)	—	—	260(SW) 210(D)	120	30
Burgundy	210(SW) 160(D)	70	10	210(D)	70	20
Rhône, Provence, South of France	210(SW) 160(D)	60	10	210(D)	100	20
Loire and Anjou	210(SW) 160(D)	100	25	210(D) 400(SW)	100(D) 200(SW)	30(D) 55(SW)
Nature et Progrès target figures for the future (to cover all regions)	—	70	0	—	70(D) 50(SP) 200(SW)	10(D) 0(SP) 35(SW)

Notes:
[1] = milligrams per litre
D = dry
SP = sparkling
SW= sweet

* = only for the very sweet French and German Wines; for normal medium and sweet wines the maximum is 260

** = This is for quality wines; for ordinary sparkling 235 mg are allowed

OTHER ADDITIVES

In addition to the additives already mentioned there may be numerous other chemicals used in the winemaking process.

There are two main objections to additives in wine. The first is the potential danger to the health of the consumer. How can we be certain that the 'safe' residue level of the chemicals is in fact safe? Every year chemicals which had previously been allowed are withdrawn from use, following new evidence of their toxicity.

The second objection is that even where the additive is thought to be utterly harmless, its use makes the wine less 'genuine' and natural. Organic wines normally contain far fewer additives in total, as well as smaller concentrations of any that are present. For reasons of consumer and environmental health, and also because they produce an individual and distinctive wine, organic alternatives can be said to be more 'genuine' and natural.

Table 5 lists additives allowed by the EC, showing their function, E number where one has been given, and also the organic ruling on them. For the organic viewpoint we have taken into account the regulations of a number of different organizations whilst relying most heavily on those of Nature et Progrès in France. This organization classifies additives and other inputs as 'recommended', 'authorized' or 'prohibited'. We have adopted this system because it conveys the relative 'enthusiasm' for the additive. The category of authorized substances is the largest, covering products which are accepted but not encouraged. Organic regulations are essentially practical, allowing the use of various inputs when necessary within the context of a philosophy based on excluding them completely if at all possible.

EC directive No. L84/52, dated 27th March 1987, and its various subsequent amendments, specified just what is allowed.

BOTTLING

Once the wine has become crystal clear, it is ready for bottling. It is very common nowadays for small producers to hire the services of a mobile bottling plant. This is a large truck which has equipment to automatically bottle the wine, put in the corks, stick foil over the bottle tops, attach front and back labels and even put the bottles into boxes and tape them up. The wine is simply pumped from the storage tank to the mobile plant — and may still be called 'Château bottled'. Even smaller producers will bottle

TABLE 5: PERMITTED ADDITIVES USED IN CONVENTIONAL WINEMAKING

Substance	'E' number	Comment	Organic viewpoint
Diammonium phosphate and Ammonium sulphate up to 0.3 g/l		To encourage yeast growth	The use of natural yeasts existing in the 'must' is recommended
Ammonium sulphate or bisulphite up to 0.3 g/l		As above	As above
Thiamin hydrochloride up to 0.6 mg/l		As above	As above
Charcoal to a maximum of 100 g of dry product		Used to correct the colour of certain white wines	'Black' carbon is forbidden; natural carbon permitted for treatment of specific wines only (e.g. Alsace, Crémants)
Sorbic acid up to 200 mg/l	E200	A preservative against mould and acts to adjust acidity levels in wine by killing some wild yeasts	Forbidden
Potassium sorbate	E202	Made from sorbic acid and has the same functions	Forbidden
Sulphur dioxide	E220-E227	Preserving and sterilizing agent. Causes headaches, stomach aches and possible allergic reactions. See Table 4	Permitted in restricted amounts and forms only. Alkaline metabisulphites are prohibited as are sulphurous solutions with more than 8% SO_2. Minimum use is recommended
Tartaric acid	E334	To increase acidity of wine where insufficient for balance of flavour	Forbidden except in the Midi region only; added to the 'must', where it may be used under the supervision of a specialist when there is no alternative way of preserving the quality of the wine. Only lead-free tartaric acid may be used

Substance	'E' number	Comment	Organic viewpoint
Natural potassium tartrate	E336	To decrease acidity	Not recommended. Permission may be granted by the control organization after analysis of the wine
Potassium bicarbonate		To decrease acidity. Synthetically made	Not authorized
Calcium carbonate	E170	To decrease acidity	Forbidden unless justified by analysis of the wine and agreed by the organic control organization
Calcium tartrate		To decrease acidity	As above
Aleppo pine resin		Used to flavour 'Retsina' Greek wines; originally with a preservative function	Natural resin would probably be allowed
Polyvinylpoly-pyrrolidone up to 80 g/l		To remove tannins from wine	Forbidden
Lactic bacteria		To convert malic to lactic acid	Permitted
Ascorbic acid up to 150 mg/l	E300	Vitamin C. Acts as an anti-oxidant and stabilizer	Forbidden
Citric acid	E330	Stabilizer. Residual amount in the finished wine must not exceed 1 g/l	Synthetic citric acid is forbidden. Natural is allowed to a maximum of 190 mg/l (one fifth of EC permitted level) and only as an alternative to the addition of SO_2 at the time of bottling
Malic Acid	296	To alter acidity levels	Not normally permitted
Calcium phytate		As above for red wines	Permitted but not recommended
Gum Arabic	E414	Stabilizer, especially of colour in red wines	Forbidden, except in quantities of 20 g/l maximum for red wines only and when necessary to stabilize the colour

Substance	'E' number	Comment	Organic viewpoint
Potassium alginate and Sodium alginate	E402 E401	From a seaweed base, used to precipitate calcium in place of metatartaric acid	Forbidden
Potassium bitartrate		To precipate tartar	Not authorized
Copper sulphate residues not to exceed 1 mg/l		To eliminate defects of smell or taste in wine	Forbidden
Caramel	E150	Added to reinforce the colour of liqueur wines. Its safety is questionable as it is available in different forms	Forbidden except for cognac and Armagnac where it is allowed

using a hand machine.

After bottling, the wine is ready for sale or further storage.

MAKING RED OR WHITE WINES

Organic or otherwise, there are important differences in the production of white and red wines. To produce white wines the grapes are pressed and the juice alone is put into the fermentation tank. For red wines the grapes are crushed and the resulting juice, skins, pips and stalks all go into the vat to ferment. This explains why the wines have different colours. All grape juice is white; but when black grape skins are left in the juice they turn it red. So, it is possible to make white wine from black grapes (Champagne being the most famous example) but not red wine from white grapes.

The skins, pips and stalks contain elements other than colour which are desirable in a red wine. The most important of these is tannin, a chemical that can make your teeth feel furry and your mouth pucker. Tannin is essential to help red wine to mature and to provide 'structure'. It also helps to combat the possibility of oxidation which can turn wine to vinegar. Its presence lessens as the wine ages, losing its bitter harshness, and becoming softer and smoother. Indeed, tannin is beneficial if the wine is not intended to be drunk for many years to come. If, however, the red wine is for more immediate drinking, it is preferable not to have too much.

White wines are, with the exception of some of the great, sweet whites, mostly made to drink young and fresh. Unlike reds, they are not improved by tannin. Nowadays highly sophisticated equipment allows white wines to be fermented at low temperatures over a relatively long period of up to six weeks. This greatly helps to produce fresh, fruity, concentrated flavours and a nice bouquet. Red wines, on the other hand, will be fermented at a much higher temperature for a shorter period. A skilful winemaker is needed in order to get the required result. In the Beaujolais region of France, red wines are made using a special technique. This involves filling the fermentation vat with carbon dioxide gas and then adding whole bunches of unpressed grapes. The fermentation starts inside the grape, which then bursts — a process which is called 'carbonic maceration'. The style of wine created in this way is the hallmark of Beaujolais — soft, fruity, light and very pleasant to drink. It will not, however, improve greatly if kept.

ROSÉ WINES

Rosé wines are not usually made by mixing up a little red with some white as one might have expected, but by leaving the white juice in contact with black grape skins for a very short period — just a few hours — so that it becomes just slightly coloured. They are then vinified in much the same way as white wine. Apart from well known wines such as Mateus Rosé from Portugal and perhaps Rosé D'Anjou from the Loire in France, there is, rather sadly, not a great demand for Rosé in the UK.

SPARKLING WINES

Sparkling wines can also be made in a variety of ways. The least impressive is simply by injecting carbon dioxide into the wine, the same method used to make soft drinks fizzy. The best sparkling wines always come from the method used in the Champagne region of France. Here the initial wine is made like a normal white wine. Subsequently it is bottled and a small dose of unfermented juice is added. A secondary fermentation then takes place in the bottle, producing carbon dioxide gas which is trapped inside, and which gives the wine its fizz. This technique is followed in many other regions of France, producing such wines as Crémant de Bourgogne and sparkling Saumur. The fine Cava wines from near Barcelona in Spain are made in the same way, and the 'champagne method', or Méthode Champenoise, is now used all over the world. But only wines actually from the Champagne region of France may be called Champagne. The use of the term 'Champagne Method' is due to be phased out, as the Champagne lobby wants to preserve its exclusive image. We will soon have to look for the words 'Fermented in the bottle' as an indication that the wine is made in the same way as Champagne. Although there is no doubt something unique about the quality of sparkling wine made in Champagne itself, there are many very good 'Méthode Champenoise' wines available at less than half the price.

SWEET WINES

Sweet wines, organic and conventional, can be processed in a number of different ways too — by stopping the fermentation while there is still natural sugar left in the juice; by adding sweet unfermented grape juice to the otherwise dry wine after fermentation as they do in Germany; or by making use of a fungus found naturally on grapes called Botrytis, or 'Noble rot'. It is called 'noble' because if it attacks grapes of the right type in the right place, at the right time, it produces some of the world's greatest sweet white wines. Sauternes, Barsac and Monbazillac from France are examples. The rot reduces the water content, leaving a shrivelled-up grape, with very concentrated sugars, able to produce very heavy rich wine.

SWEET GERMAN WINES

In Germany the best quality wines are graded according to the sugar content of the grapes in the 'must' prior to fermentation. Starting with Kabinett (named as such because these were good wines kept by the producer for personal use in his Cabinet), the traditional 'lieblich' style become progressively sweeter and more concentrated in flavour as the grading progresses. Spätlese — meaning late picked, and thus riper and containing more sugar; Auslese — specially selected bunches of late picked grapes; Berenauslese — individually selected super-ripe grapes affected by 'Noble Rot'; Trockenberenauslese — wines in which the grapes have dried (trocken) on the vine and are thus even more concentrated in sugar; and finally Eiswein — this is made from grapes that have been left on the vines until after the first frost, so that the juice freezes in the grapes, making them even sweeter.

Kabinett quality wines are reasonably easy to find on sale in the UK; Spätlese and Auslese can be found if you look for them, but the rest require searching out. They can become very expensive, but if your pocket can stretch to it, do get some good advice from a local merchant about which is the best on offer at the time and treat yourself!

3

HOW DO WE KNOW IT'S ORGANIC?

What guarantee has the consumer got that wine sold as organic is, in fact, genuinely organic? It has to be said that at present the situation is confusing to the 'person in the street'.

Most organic winemakers belong to inspection schemes which set down rigid rules defining how the grapes should be grown and the wine made. Only certain substances are allowed, as referred to in the previous chapter. Along with the rules goes a control system involving regular inspections of the growers to make sure that they are adhering to the regulations.

A wine producer joining an organic association is bound by the rules of that body. A formal contract is signed which is renewable annually. The producer must make his or her whole operation open to inspection by the association. The soil and the wine are analysed, and the paperwork is checked. The producer must pay a subscription to the organization (usually related to turnover), and in turn may use their logo on the wine label as evidence that the wine is 'verified' as organic.

This system is really the only way of being sure that the wine is genuinely organic. The identifying logo ties the contents of the bottle to a particular set of rules and controls.

ORGANIC VERIFICATION SCHEMES

There is, unfortunately, no single inspection scheme for all organic wines. Consequently, the consumer is presented with a confusing array of logos and statements of organic authenticity which may or may not appear on the bottle. In France alone there are sixteen different sets of standards to which a producer can adhere.

Although most of the organic organizations of different nations belong to the international co-ordinating body, IFOAM (International Federation of Organic Agriculture Movements) and share essentially the same approach, there are inevitably differences in the details of their recommended production methods. Such differences exist because of varying technical and scientific opinions, and because what is appropriate to making organic wine in one particular climate or country is not in another.

Also, within the same organic association, regulations may vary occasionally according to the region and the style of wine being produced. The aim is always to make the most natural and chemical-free product possible, whilst at the same time maintaining the quality of the wine. The use of sulphur dioxide is perhaps the clearest example of this. Quantities permitted by organic standards vary according to the type of wine, with sweet whites being allowed to contain higher levels than red wines.

In another case, Nature et Progrès, the largest organic organization in France, strictly prohibit the addition of tartaric acid in all wines, except in the Midi region of southern France in very specific circumstances. The grapes in this region sometimes lack sufficient natural acidity to produce a well-made 'balanced' wine. Tartaric acid, which occurs naturally and provides acidity, may be added to the 'must' of the wine and even then in controlled amounts following the advice of an oenologue (specialist winemaker) when there is absolutely no alternative.

The following is not a definitive list of all organic organizations. It contains the larger bodies and all those which appear in this book. For comprehensive details of the national organizations in each country, contact the international body which acts as a co-ordinator:

IFOAM (International Federation of Organic Agriculture Movements), c/o Olkozentrum Imsbach, D-6695 Tholey-Theley, Germany.

NB: IFOAM is not a rule maker in its own right.

NATIONAL ORGANIZATIONS

France

There is a wide variety of organic organizations in France, of which the three biggest are Nature et Progrès, UNIA and FESA. The reason there are so many is only in part to do with technical or scientific differences; in fact the essential regulations are very

similar, the rulebook of Nature et Progrès being the most comprehensive source. The differences stem from personality and regional
conflicts, and historical evolution. The largest organization,
Nature et Progrès, grew out of consumer concerns after the 1968
period of student rebellion. UNIA and FESA both have their
origins in producer groups, originating from the organization set
up by the two founding fathers Messieurs Lemaire and Boucher,
whose Lemaire-Boucher organization has now been replaced by
UNIA. Several wines of older vintages listed in Part Two have the
Lemaire-Boucher logo on the bottle; we have listed these as UNIA
in the text, as this is the name of the organization the wine producer
now belongs to. UNIA is mostly, though not exclusively, found in
the south of France, where FESA has little or no representation.
Many of the other smaller groups are also regionally-based. Where
a winemaker is in the transition from chemical use to full organic
status, it is normal to find this indicated by words such as 'en
reconversion' next to the name of the organization.

The French Government-sponsored logo, AB for Agriculture
Biologique, has not yet come into use for wines, as it is currently
restricted to unprocessed products, such as grapes. When it does,
it will appear alongside the logo of the organic association to which
the winemaker belongs.

Commonly Seen on Wine Labels

PRODUCTION DE L'AGRICULTURE BIOLOGIQUE

cultivée sans engrais chimiques, ni pesticides organiques de synthèse

conformément au Cahier des Charges de la F.E.S.A.
membre du C.I.N.A.B.

PRODUIT DE L'AGRICULTURE BIOLOGIQUE
Cultivé par un Membre de
NATURE & PROGRÈS

Nature et Progrès
FESA = Fédération Européenne des Syndicats d'Agrobiologistes
(also known by their logo 'Terre et Vie')
UNIA = Union Nationale Interprofessionnelle de l'Agrobiolo-
gie (incorporating the Méthode Lemaire-Boucher)
EAP = Environnement–Alimentation–Progrès
FNAB BIOFRANC = Fédération Nationale de l'Agriculture
Biologique
BIOPLAMPAC = Association Inter-Régionale des Agrobiolo-
gistes du Quart Sud-Ouest de la France
Groupement d'Agrobiologistes
Paysan Agrobiologiste
Demeter (Biodynamic Association)
Dynorga (Biodynamic trademark of M Daumas in the Rhône
and with few other adherents at present)

Italy

Things are moving apace in the Italian organic movement. In such
a huge and unregulated country there are probably a large number
of small 'independent' organic growers. There are also a lot of very
small 'verified' producers whose output is not sufficient to sell
commercially. The most important organization at present is the
Associazione Italiana per l'Agricoltura Biologica, founded in 1988.
It is an umbrella organization with some 900 associated producers
in total, of whom only a handful are making wine in commercial
quantities. AIAB membership is composed of other organic
organizations, often regional, who in turn have individual
producer members. Two or three times a year regional inspectors
carry out inspections on the producers. The national organization
conducts spot checks over and above those carried out by the
regional officials. Individual growers can thus belong to both a
regional and national body for their certification. Heightened
concern over environmental issues generally has enabled the
organic lobby in some regions to win financial backing from
governmental sources to fund the inspectorate system.

Commonly Seen on Wine Labels

AIAB = Associazione Italiana per l'Agricoltura Biologica
Suolo e Salute
Demeter
Biodyn (the conversion stage for Demeter)

Germany

As in France and Italy, there are numerous small regional groups.
However, the biggest and most important national organization for
wine producers is the Bundesverband Okologischer Weinbau
which has about 100 of the 130 or so verified growers amongst its
membership. Many wine producers belong to this organization and
one other. Identification of German organic wines is difficult
because it is not permitted to use the words organic, or the German
equivalent 'Biologische', on the wine label. It is permissible,
however, to state the name of the organic organization to which the
producer belongs.

Commonly Seen on Wine Labels

Bundesverband Okologischer Weinbau
Arbeitsgemeinschaft für Naturnahen Obst-, Gemüse-, und Feldfruchtanbau
Bioland
Naturland
Ring Okologisch Arbeitender Winzer Rheinhessen

Rest of the World
Other countries have fewer organic organizations. Those appearing on wines featured in this book are:

Vida Sana (Spain)

Umbella (Spain)

AGROBIO = Associaçao Portugesa de Agricultura Biológica (Portugal)

BIOGROW = New Zealand Biological Producers' Council (New Zealand)

NASAA = National Association for Sustainable Agriculture (Australia)

California Certified Organic Growers (USA)

EKO = Stichting Ekomerk Control (Holland), the body which verifies Hungarian wines.

In Britain a common set of organic standards has been established by the Government-funded autonomous body Food From Britain. In 1986 it set up the United Kingdom Register of Organic Food Standards (UKROFS) which after several years of discussion came up with a document largely based on the Soil Association (SA) standards. The Soil Association is the UK's largest and best-known organic standards organization. At present there are only two commercial winemakers in Britain growing to organic standards, both of them Soil Association approved. Like the AB symbol in France, the UKROFS symbol is not granted to processed foods and drink at present.

INDEPENDENT PRODUCERS

Not everyone producing organic wine belongs to an inspection scheme. There is a not inconsiderable number of so-called 'independent' organic producers. They claim to make organic wine and in many cases follow the standards laid down by formal bodies except that they do not actually join the scheme.

The problem with independent organic producers is that there are no controls or checks on their production methods. This is not to imply that they are charlatans. Many are small, fiercely independent growers, who resent having to defer to an outside body.

That independent producers are able to sell wine as organic without being required to subject their wares to inspection is clearly unsatisfactory. Happily for the consumer, this situation is soon to change when regulations defining organic production methods are introduced by the EC. These will make it an offence in law to sell produce labelled as organic unless the farmer or grower belongs to an approved symbol-awarding organization. Draft regulations covering the production of cereals, vegetables and other field crops (though not wine) are currently under consideration. Hopefully within the next few years all produce labelled organic will be brought under such controls. Until then it is best to stick to wines that have been properly authenticated by the organic movement.

ACCIDENTAL CONTAMINATION

It should be stressed that all organic standards refer to the way in which grapes are grown and wine made. They do not, and indeed cannot, offer a guarantee to the public that organic wines will be entirely free from pesticides.

It is an unfortunate fact of 20th-century life that we live in a highly-polluted environment. Many chemicals may find their way into a wine by chance. Unintentional pollution, whether high nitrate levels in water, acid rain or radiation poisoning from Chernobyl, all unbeknown to us, are tainting our food and drink. For the organic winemaker close to a neighbour spraying chemicals, there is always the danger of wind blowing the spray over on to his organic vines. For this reason many organic growers will deliberately choose an isolated site, away from others — perhaps protected by a range of trees or hill or away from arterial roads and the exhaust emissions of vehicles.

Potentially hazardous chemicals can, therefore, find their way into the soil. Traces of forbidden substances may still be found in a vineyard which has been adhering strictly to organic methods for years, simply because it can take a very long time for the soil to be completely 'cleaned'. Vines, which send roots far down into the ground, might still find chemical residues.

A very strict organic grower in Bordeaux was found to have pesticide residues in his wine. Knowing that he had never used pesticides, he sought to clear his name. He eventually discovered that the source of the chemical was the corks he used, which had been treated with insecticide to protect them from rotting. Some of this pesticide had been passed into the wine in the bottle. He changed to using untreated corks immediately.

Organic organizations constantly seek to refine and enlarge their standards, so that situations like this become less and less frequent. Continual developments in the chemicals used necessitate ever-greater precision by organic winemakers.

— 4 —
READING THE LABEL

Many people are frightened of wine. It appears to be part of a rather glamorous and mysterious world, one which is often intimidating to ordinary people. The increasingly large range of bottles on the retailer's shelf is indeed an imposing sight. No longer are we faced with a simple choice of French, German or Italian wines. From all over the world, wines jostle for our attention — Australian, Californian, Russian and even Chilean, all sit proudly alongside their European cousins.

We can also choose wine from a particular region, grape variety and year. Change any one of these three factors, and the resulting wine will taste different. Although these are only some of the parameters that determine the taste and style of a wine, they are the only ones identifiable on the label at present.

So how can you find out precisely what kind of wine you are buying? Start with the label. Learn how to interpret and evaluate it. To know that the wine with the rather elegant-looking gold and black label declares itself as being made in 1988, from Merlot and Syrah grapes, in a region of southern France called Oc, may not leave you any the wiser. But if you know the styles of red wine which are common in this region, whether or not 1988 was a year with good quality grapes and well-made wines, whether the combination of Merlot and Syrah here is likely to produce a wine to drink now or leave for several years — then you can make a more informed decision. Nowadays many retailers, especially specialist merchants, go to considerable lengths to provide information about the style and taste of each wine. Some will even let you taste before you buy. If the staff are knowledgeable and enthusiastic, a lot can be learnt and a great deal of pleasure derived by shopping in the right place.

But for the busy consumer, often buying wine in a supermarket, the facts are harder to come by. A few years ago the Wine Development Board introduced the 1—9 grading system for white wines to make life easier for the amateur wine buyer. Number 1 denotes the driest types of wine, and number 9 the sweetest. This is a very generalized and rough guide, but it is at least intelligible — which is more than can be said for many other aspects of the wine trade. These codes have been incorporated into our wine guide in Part Two.

Similarly, the basic but instructive details on the back labels of wine bottles can provide a very simple but understandable description. To be informed that the wine is a very dry, crisp white, is useful if you in fact want a semi-sweet sparkling wine, and have no other means of telling one bottle from another. The information on a back label is, however, brief and is sometimes less than specific — the all-encompassing 'suitable on its own or with a wide variety of foods' must surely be the wine world's best entry for the 'Great Empty Phrases of Our Time' Award. While we might learn about the type of product from the information given on the label, we are told very little about the actual contents of the bottle — there are no ingredients listed.

WHAT YOU'RE NOT TOLD ON THE LABEL

We looked at the differences between organic and 'chemical wines' in earlier chapters. What wine labels do not tell us at present is the difference in the finished product because of these two different approaches to winemaking. If they did, we would expect the labels of most bulk-produced chemical wines to show a long list of the chemicals added during the winemaking process, plus perhaps the unwanted residues of chemicals used on the grapes during their cultivation. Organic wines would show a vastly smaller number of additives, perhaps including sulphur dioxide or natural citric acid.

Ideally, all wine, irrespective of whether it is made from organically-grown grapes, should declare any additives used during winemaking and should also list any pesticides or other chemicals introduced to the vineyard. The list might even include fining or clarifying agents, such as isinglass and egg whites; these are harmless and not present in the finished wine, but the information might nonetheless be useful to vegetarians or vegans.

Declarations need to be matched by random checking and analysis to try to ensure that what is said to be in the wine — or not in it — is actually the case. Without an efficient system of control there is no way of knowing that the information on the labels is in fact accurate.

Ingredient labelling of wine has progressed further in the USA and Australia than anywhere else. US wines now have to carry a Government health warning similar to that on cigarette packets in the UK. It says 'Government Warning: According to the Surgeon General, women should not drink alcoholic beverages during pregnancy because of the risk of birth defects. Consumption of alcoholic beverages impairs your ability to drive a car or operate machinery, and may cause health problems.' Both US and Australian wines have to declare sulphur dioxide (in whatever form it has been used) on the bottle. The labels state 'contains sulfites' in the USA and 'Contains Preservative E220' in Australia. 'E Nos 221-7, part of the sulphur group', may also appear. Australian wines also list antioxidants such as E300 (ascorbic acid or vitamin C).

However, the regulations governing ingredients listing in the USA and Australia only apply to bottles consumed within those countries. Wines exported by them to the UK are covered by UK regulations, which do not require such listings. We checked a number of American and Australian wines in British stores and found that some have the additives listed clearly, whilst some do not. Some have the listing deliberately covered over with another label, usually bearing the name of the importer. Obviously some exporters and UK retailers believe that consumers would be put off wine that contains additives. The legislation in the USA produced a furore of opposition and comment from the wine trade, both there and in the UK, because it downgraded the image of wine and was thought to be bad for marketing. They still want people to believe that wine is a 'natural' product!

The more sophisticated opposition argue that not all wine is equally processed, and that great estates such as Château-Lafite or Margaux should not be grouped under the same umbrella as cheap, mass-produced, and much more chemicalized 'plonk'! Maybe so, but if we had a more comprehensive and detailed label the consumer would be able to tell at a glance which wines are 'natural' and which are not. In fact, astute producers of quality wines may come to realize that the more detailed the labelling, the better for them. If they do not use lots of 'nasties' it's a good reason for demanding a good price. Producers not using chemicals in the vineyard or the winery should welcome the ingredients listings, which would declare their wine free of such products. A reticence to do so can only imply that unwelcome chemicals have been used. Those with nothing to hide should be proud to declare it!

WHAT YOU ARE TOLD

The Name of the Wine

On bottles of French wine you may see a name such as 'Château Renaissance' or 'Domaine de L'Ile'; in Germany it might be something like 'Weingut Gebruder Müller' (the wine estate of the Müller brothers); in New Zealand or the USA, 'Millton Vineyard' or 'Frey Vineyard'. Château, Domaine, Weingut, Vineyard — all indicate that these wines come from the property mentioned rather than being the product of several vineyards.

You will often find the origin indicated on both the label of the wine and the side of the cork. It is presumed to be superior, because it shows that the wine comes from one particular producer, rather than from a whole number of growers who then have their wines blended by a third party before bottling. While this is generally true — especially in the upper echelons of the wine world — there are now many extremely good co-operatives and négociants (the third party, which blends and bottles the wines). The word 'Château' covers everything from the grandest Bordeaux mansion to a tiny modern house with a few vines planted over the road. In fact the words Château and Domaine simply refer to a specific property, the land and the building, where the wine is made. The use of these titles is officially sanctioned; some properties have the right to use both Domaine and Château names, or several different Château names, for wines from exactly the same place!

Region

High quality wines will often indicate the area of a country that the wine comes from, such as Burgundy in France, Rheinpfalz in Germany, Barossa Valley in Australia, or Chianti in Italy. The region can be a large area, as with Bordeaux, or tiny, down to a specific village. Where the region is better known than the producer, this may become the main name on the label. This is very common in Burgundy (Bourgogne), for example, where 'Hautes Côtes de Nuits' will often be in bolder letters rather than the property name in many cases. The same is often true for middle-range quality wines. In southern France, Vin de Pays wines from regions such as the Hérault, Aude, or Oc often have the region as the main identifying mark, possibly combined with the grape type. This may be because the wine does not come from one estate and so cannot use a single estate name, but it may also be because the region the wine comes from is better known and thus more marketable ('Vin de Pays de l'Aude' simply meaning 'wine from the region of Aude').

Bottler/Producer

The most significant factor here is whether or not the wine is bottled where the grapes are grown. Again, this does not guarantee better quality, but it is considered more prestigious, partly because it is more specific. English-speaking countries will usually have 'estate bottled' or similar. In France 'Mis en bouteille à la propriété' or 'Mis en bouteille au Château/Domaine' are common indications and other countries have their equivalent. German wines carry a long number which is the quality testing number given after the wine has been approved. When the wine has been bottled by someone other than the grower/producer, it will say 'Bottled by' and then the name of the person or company. This enables identification of a wine which does not have a specific property name. For example, there are lots of 'Vin de Pays de Gascogne' available. They do not all taste the same, and if they fail to carry a property or name, we must see who bottled the wine in order to identify it further. However, 'generic' wine like this could well include wine from many different growers and blends, all sold under identical labels. If produced and/or bottled by one company it should at least be consistent in style. Large bottlers and négociants of this type can establish a reputation for a particular quality and style of a wine. The overwhelming majority of organic wines are bottled on the estate of the grower and producer.

Grape Type

If the wine is made from just one or two grape varieties and the grapes are well-known, they are often put on the label. So look out for 'Chardonnay', 'Sauvignon', 'Gewürztraminer' among the French whites, 'Müller-Thurgau', 'Scheurebe', 'Riesling' for German whites; and 'Cabernet Sauvignon', 'Merlot', 'Pinot Noir' amongst the reds of many countries. Sometimes there are two grapes listed on the label, as in the very successful Australian blend of Cabernet Sauvignon and Shiraz (the former being the larger proportion). Sometimes the percentage of each is given. In EC countries a wine stating a single grape variety must contain at least 85 per cent of that grape; in New Zealand and California it must be 75 per cent, allowing the addition of 25 per cent of a usually cheaper, higher yielding variety. In Australia the grape stated on the label must constitute 80 per cent of the total contents.

Vintage

If a quality wine is produced from grapes grown in a specific year, it will probably be mentioned on the label. Note that under most regulations the year indicates when the grapes were harvested, not when the wine was bottled. Remember that older does not necessarily mean better — in fact probably the opposite for fresh dry whites. Each vintage or year of a wine will have its own particular flavour and style — its character. Each region will have 'good', 'average' and 'bad' years; in other words, when the climate was more or less favourable to the production of the wine. In the 1980s in Bordeaux for example, 1987 was generally regarded as a 'bad' vintage for red wines. Quite a lot of quality wine producers did not even consider their wine good enough to bottle under their own name. Instead they chose to maintain the quality and image of their estate by selling the 1987 wine cheaply in bulk for blending with other wines, or for local consumption. But while this was the overall picture, there is still plenty of good 1987 red Bordeaux around. So it is necessary to be precise in assessing the merits of each vintage and wine. The words for vintage, or harvest, to look out for on the labels are: 'Récolte' (French), 'Cosecha' (Spanish) or 'Vendemmia' (Italian).

Quality Marks

In the main European wine-producing countries there are official categories for wine quality. In France there are four gradings which appear on the wine label, starting with 'Vin de Table' as the most basic and progressing through 'Vin de Pays', 'Vin Délimité de Qualité Supérieure' and finally 'Appellation Contrôlée'. The last, abbreviated as AC or AOC on the label, means that the wine comes from the geographical area shown on the label (except in the case of Muscadet, which is a grape type). It is generally assumed that within any particular region the smaller and more specific the locality of the AC area, the better and more prestigious the wine will be. There are therefore large regions, such as Bordeaux, or small specific locations, such as Châteauneuf-du-Pape in the southern

Rhône valley, or Puligny Montrachet in Burgundy.

There are also regulations governing several other factors such as which grape varieties can be used, the number of vines that can be planted, the amount of wine that can be produced and the alcohol level. To qualify for the status of Appellation Contrôlée all these rules must be adhered to in order for the AC grading to be granted. The wine will also have to be tasted and approved by the local wine authority as worthy of the name. 'Vin Délimité de Qualité Supérieure' (VDQS) has similar restrictions which are not as tight; 'Vin de Pays' is less strict still and essentially means that the wine has come from a named region. 'Vin de Table' can come from anywhere in France.

While this grading system is intended to preserve both quality and regional character, it is not in fact a guarantee of either. Producers may decide that they want to include a grape variety which is not officially authorized by the AC rules of the area. In this case they will have only 'Vin de Table' status for their wine, even if it is a superb and very expensive product. There are numerous examples of this in Provence in southern France and in Italy.

On the other hand, even when a wine qualifies for the AC designation, there is no guarantee that the viticulture and vinification have been carried out well, and the wine of high quality. A well-made 'Vin de Pays' wine could easily be of better quality than a poorly-made AC. The AC regulations provide the backcloth for making a good quality wine, they do not guarantee it.

In Germany the equivalent of the AC designation is the 'Qualitätswein' (QmP). Italy has the 'Denominazione di Origine Controllata' (e Garantia), or DOC(G), and Spain its 'Denominacion de Origen'. Many other countries do not have clear differentials leading to such quality levels, so here the reputation of the area, producer/bottler and type of wine is the only real guide — apart from experience of tasting! England is a case in point — EC wisdom classifies all English wine as table wine, however good the quality.

Apart from the items above you may also find details of some of the following:

Organic Authenticity

A full description of the standards behind the organic symbols on the label was given in Chapter 3. The most common verifiable organic logos are as follows:

PRODUCTION DE L'AGRICULTURE BIOLOGIQUE

cultivée sans engrais chimiques, ni pesticides organiques de synthèse

conformément au Cahier des Charges de la F.E.S.A.
membre du C.I.N.A.B.

 PRODUIT DE L'AGRICULTURE BIOLOGIQUE
Cultivé par un Membre de
NATURE & PROGRÈS

Liquid Content
All full bottles must contain 75cl of wine. In the past it was possible to find 70cl or 73cl bottles — quantities used because the lower contents meant less alcohol tax. As most of us merely buy a bottle, and do not scrutinize the 'contents', it seemed on the surface that the wine was cheaper. However, shaving a few centilitres off has now been banned and all wines must be the full 75cl. The volume must be stated on the label.

Alcohol Content
It is obligatory to state this on the label. It usually varies between 8 and 15 per cent.

Health Warnings
As discussed on page 55 in relation to the USA.

Additives
As discussed on page 55 in relation to the USA and Australia.

Wine Style

Sometimes the label will tell you the style of the wine. Common in France are Doux and Moelleux for sweet wines; Mousseux for sparkling; Sec and Demi-sec for dry and medium dry respectively (still wines only); and Brut, which indicates dry sparkling wines.

Awards

High quality wines win a gold medal here or a bronze medal there. Not all such competitions mean a lot — those in Paris and Mâcon are the most important ones in France.

Top Quality Wines

There are a few special high status indications, such as Cru Classé in Bordeaux, which means that the wine is from an estate ranked among the five top quality categories in the Bordeaux region.

Château le Barradis

RÉPUTÉ EN HOLLANDE DEPUIS 1530

MONBAZILLAC

APPELLATION MONBAZILLAC CONTROLÉE

13,5% vol.

75 cl

1983

PRODUCE OF FRANCE

M^r & Mme S. LABASSE - GAZZINI

VITICULTEURS A MONBAZILLAC (DORDOGNE)

MIS EN BOUTEILLES AU CHATEAU

PRODUIT DE L'AGRICULTURE BIOLOGIQUE

Cultivé par un Membre de

NATURE & PROGRÈS

Fig 2: Example of an organic wine label

Special Remarks

The title 'Grand Vin' does not actually mean this wine is grander than any other, it is just an inference by the producer that this is quality wine. Similarly 'Cuvée Spéciale', meaning special blend or perhaps best vat, may indeed actually be the best wine from a particular batch, or it may just be a marketing device. 'Terroir Privilégié' (Privileged Soil) might apply to a vineyard in a good position to receive plenty of sunlight, but it does not indicate any official privilege.

5

ENJOYING WINE

This chapter is about enjoying wine, and although the authors think personally that organic wines offer the greatest pleasure, much of the following advice also applies to conventional wine and covers buying, storing, serving, tasting and drinking wine with food. Hugh Johnson, greatest of all British wine journalists, wrote in his *World Atlas of Wine,* that 'To buy good wine and not look after it properly is like hanging a masterpiece in a dark corner, or not exercising a racehorse, or not polishing your Rolls Royce'. Very few of us can afford a Rolls Royce or to buy 'great' wines! However, many of the wines listed in this book fall into the 'good wine' category, so they need to be looked after and appreciated.

BUYING WINE

Note: The prices given in this chapter reflect those current at the time of writing in late 1990.

There are not many organic wines available at under £3.00 a bottle, due to production methods and the small scale of operation. Generally, the cheaper the wine, the bigger the difference in price between organic and conventional. An organic 'Vin de Pays' wine may cost as much as 50 per cent more than a non-organic equivalent. Add on the higher unit costs of small importers and retailers, and it can easily appear as though organic wines are significantly dearer.

The question of cost plagues organic foods. After all, it does not matter how much we want to eat and drink healthily, if we cannot afford it. Organic products are more expensive partly because labour and time-consuming techniques cost more than chemicals at present. Organic foods often retail at a higher price than conventional equivalents. The situation is different with organic wines. There is frequently no significant difference in price once the £5 or £6 a bottle mark is reached. In the £3 to £5 bracket, where many organic wines are, it is important to compare like with like. If two wines of exactly the same specification and quality are compared in the same shop, there will usually be little or no difference between organic and conventional. It is important to read the label carefully when comparing, to ensure that the wines are similar. Top quality estate-bottled 'Muscadet de Sèvre et Maine Sur Lie' will probably cost around £4.50 in a wine merchant, regardless of whether it is organic or not. Basic bulk-produced Muscadet in a supermarket may be under £2.50. To compare the price of quality organic wine with the supermarket bottle would be like comparing a Saab to a Skoda!

INVESTING IN WINE

For those who wish to buy wine to keep as an investment, there is not a great deal of scope as yet with organic wines. This sort of buying is a very specialist affair requiring skill, bravado and above all, money.

People buying fine wine to lay down purchase what they hope will become very expensive, great wines from famous Châteaux, when they are less than a year old. The price reflects the gamble they are taking. The idea is that by the time it is ready for drinking, the value of the wine will have risen sufficiently to earn the investor a pretty penny. As an example of the amounts of money involved, here is a small selection from *Decanter* magazine's 1990 Vintage guide in which they cited the *en primeur* prices available at the time, from leading UK merchants. These included £475 a case of 12 bottles of Château-Margaux (collection from the vineyard, duty, VAT, freight and ancillary costs on top), £498 from Mouton-Rothschild, or a mere £250 from Château Palmer. While 1989 was indeed a very fine vintage in general, and properties such as these are amongst the best in the world, it is clearly an arena for the wealthy. How long will it be, we wonder, before there is a market for *en primeur* organic claret?

THE DEMAND FOR ORGANIC WINE

Organic wine consumption in Britain was, until just a few years ago, a minority interest. Over on the Continent things were different, with the Germans, stimulated by their desire for post-Chernobyl pollution-free products, consuming more organic wine than the rest of Europe put together. Surprisingly, the French and Italians, though major producers of organic wine, do not yet have a large domestic market for organic wine *per se:* most of their production goes abroad.

Interest in drinking organic wines, because they are organic, comes principally from Northern Europe — Germany, Holland and ourselves. Demand in the UK has increased dramatically in the recent past — albeit from small beginnings — as the number of retailers stocking organic wines has grown. The National Organic Wine Fair which is held annually at Ryton Gardens, near Coventry, in July is one of the few genuine consumer wine fairs in the UK. Organized by the Henry Doubleday Research Association, at the National Centre for Organic Gardening, it is both a stimulant and testimony to the growing demand for organic wines. Safeway plc saw the benefit of sponsoring the Fair in its second year and have not regretted the decision. In its fourth year in 1991, the Fair goes from strength to strength.

Elsewhere in the world importing countries now include Switzerland, Denmark, Luxembourg, the USA, Canada and Japan.

DUTIES AND TAXES

When buying any wine, it is worth remembering that the more you pay, the higher the proportion of the price for the wine itself rather than for taxes and other costs. One of the chief of these is excise, or alcohol duty.

The cost of the alcohol duty varies according to the amount of wine in the bottle and its alcohol content, and not to the quality or price of the wine. Most 'still' table wines are between 8 and 15 degrees alcohol and all carry the same alcohol tax. If the wine is higher than 15 degrees — as is normal for sherry or port, for example — the tax increases considerably. Sparkling wines also carry a higher tax. Litre or 2-litre bottles are taxed pro rata. Finally, wine from outside the EC is subject to a customs tax of about 8p per 75cl bottle (plus VAT).

How these taxes translate into the price of a bottle of wine becomes clear if we look at how the costs of two different bottles are made up. One costs £2.29, the other £5.49. Both come from within the EC, are in 75cl bottles, are 'still' rather than sparkling, and have an alcoholic strength of between 9 per cent and 15 per cent.

TABLE 6: BREAKDOWN OF WINE COST

	Wine at £2.29	Wine at £5.49
	£	£
Wine	0.45	2.50
VAT	0.30	0.72
Excise (alcohol duty)	0.83	0.83
Shipping/storage	0.20	0.20
Retailers margin 35% on all costs (ex. VAT)	0.51	1.24
Total	£2.29	£5.49

As a proportion of the total, the cost of the wine forms just under 20 per cent for the bottle costing £2.29, but not far short of 50 per cent for the bottle costing £5.49. And the cost of the wine includes not just the liquid but also the bottles, corks, capsules, labels, boxes and pallets the wine is shipped on. Once all these are taken into account the wine in the cheaper bottle might as well be free! What this says about its likely quality is obvious.

Of course, it may be that the retailer's margin is lower than 35 per cent for the cheaper wine, so the wine element may in fact be a little higher. The figures in Table 6 are just a guide. Retailers' margins vary quite a lot. There may also be the margin of the importer to add to the equation if the wine is not shipped direct from the producer but bought from a company with stocks already in the UK. Similarly, if the same wine is bought in a restaurant it will cost even more: the normal restaurant margin is at least 100 per cent, and in expensive areas such as central London it will be very much more.

It is well worth 'trading up' when eating out, as there tends to be a higher margin put on house wines than on the better quality wines. In terms of value for money then, if you can afford it, it is probably better to spend £10 a bottle for a Château bottled wine, rather than £6.75 on the house 'plonk'. But again, it's a matter of knowing the individual restaurant or wine bar. Some very laudable owners have cottoned on to the fact that we do not like paying through the nose for our wines when eating out, and charge a flat rate on the cost. They may decide to put, say, £3 on every bottle regardless of price. This certainly encourages the buying of better wines!

TO DRINK OR TO KEEP?

It is a common error to think that the older a wine is, the better. This is not necessarily so. It entirely depends on the type of wine and how it has been made. A dry white made for drinking fresh will probably have gone stale in flavour and possibly will have begun to oxidize after two or three years. A good full-bodied red or sweet white probably will benefit from keeping for several years, depending on the style of wine and the vintage. Each year has its own character and qualities, and it is perfectly possible for a wine made in, say, 1988 to be better for drinking long before a wine made in 1986 from the same estate. This is currently the case with many red Bordeaux. When a wine is said to be 'young' this is not just, or even necessarily, a reference to the fact that it was made recently. It is a judgement on the stage of development of that particular vintage of wine. The 1988 might well have reached its middle age while the 1986 is still at primary school; and the '88 may not live as long as the '86.

One of the best ways to learn about the effect of time on wine is to buy half a dozen bottles of a red wine from a single estate, and of a specific vintage, that will keep well. Hide them away, and drink a bottle, at more or less the same time, each year. Keep a notebook and write down your comments on the colour, smell and taste of the wine on each occasion. If you choose a wine which matures quite quickly (i.e. one which will have changed considerably over a 6-year period), the development will be easier to spot. Even better, repeat this experiment with several wines from the same region, but from different estates, so that you can not only compare the development of a wine from one particular estate, but also the differences in development between the wines of several.

STORING WINE

Storing wine is not a complicated business: it is simply a matter of finding the right conditions. Wine that is going to be drunk within a few months of purchase does not need special treatment. However, all wine should be kept out of the light and at a constant temperature —ideally between 7 and 15 degrees Celsius. Never buy a bottle of wine that has been on display under a fluorescent light in a shop window! It will probably not be at its best after exposure to concentrated light, and warm temperatures. The ideal place to store wine that is being kept for any length of time, is an old cellar, where it is not subject to movement, rapid changes of temperature or bright light. Today's centrally heated houses can be a problem if the wine is being heated and cooled twice a day — treatment that will not improve it!

Wine being kept for several years after bottling should be laid down on its side so that the cork is always kept moist; otherwise it may dry out, shrink, and not seal the wine against the air. A most expensive claret may become very expensive vinegar! This is the origin of the term 'laying down' a wine — storing it correctly on its side while it matures.

You should also avoid storing strong-smelling cheeses and strings of garlic near to your wine.

The Taste of Organic Wine?

Can you tell if a wine is organic by its taste? Do organic wines taste better? There isn't an identifiable organic flavour or style because, as we mentioned in Chapter 1, there is a range of factors governing the flavour of any wine. People often remark that organic fruit, vegetables and meat have a much stronger, fuller flavour than their chemical counterparts. Observers have said that organic wines have more individuality, and are perhaps fruitier. But really fullness of flavour and individuality are the marks of a well-made, rather than just an organic, wine. Being organic provides the launching pad to achieving a high overall quality. On the other hand, it is easier to tell a wine that is definitely not organic when you can taste the presence of a large amount of sulphur dioxide.

WINE TASTING

How can you taste wines without falling into the trap of becoming completely esoteric when describing them? The much-ridiculed caricature of the droning old wine bore fits in well with the traditional view of wine. The ridicule is no doubt entirely justified; it is nevertheless essential for people in the trade, and also wine enthusiasts, to be able to discuss and describe wines so that other people can understand the tastes and smells they are trying to convey. But does the language really have to be so overblown and exaggerated that it sometimes actually clouds rather than clarifies the understanding of the wine?

There are a number of commonly-used terms that serve to increase understanding of the style and quality of a wine. We use these phrases — such as 'length', 'nicely balanced', 'full-bodied' — in our descriptions in Part Two, and explain them in the Glossary.

Arranging a Tasting

If you are arranging a tasting with friends, it is probably most enjoyable to pick a theme. This might be wines all made from the same grape, such as Sauvignon. Then you can readily taste the diversity of flavours and styles that a single grape can produce, in the different countries and regions of the world. Or you might choose a style of wine — light, fruity reds or richly sweet dessert wines, for example — with samples from different countries and regions. As you become more experienced you can make the parameters more specific, perhaps choosing a number of wines from different producers in, say, the St Emilion region of Bordeaux all made in the same year, or all from the same Château but from several different vintages. The number of wines to taste is entirely optional, but 6 to 8 is typical. Professional tasters will frequently taste up to 50 wines in a session, but this is usually when they are looking for something particular to buy and, because they have a lot of tasting experience, can quickly discern one from another.

Choosing the Right Glasses

The choice of the glass is not just an affectation; it does make a difference to the appreciation of the wine. It is, therefore, worth trying to ensure that the glasses you choose are suitable for the job. There is an ideal glass for just about every kind of wine, but the easiest and cheapest solution is to choose a tulip-shaped one. This shape allows you to swirl the wine around a bit — necessary for aerating the wine and releasing the fullness of the smell and flavour, without spilling it all over your hands. Or go one better and use the International Standardization Organization (ISO) glass, specially designed for tasting wine, and now quite readily available. Both of these glasses are wider in the middle and narrow towards the top, allowing for both swirling of the liquid and a better chance of the smell lingering for a while.

The Serving Order

Most tastings start with white wines and then go on to reds, but it can be the other way round. The norm is to start with the driest white and progress through medium to end up with the sweetest. This is just common sense, because it is hard to properly taste a dry after a sweet. Reds, which are almost always dry, start with the lightest and end up with the most full-bodied.

Temperature

If the white wines are chilled this is best done lightly, because the colder the wine, the less you can appreciate the flavour. This is worth remembering if you are stuck with a pretty ordinary wine to give out at a meal or party — chill it to death and disguise its humble status! Otherwise whites can be profitably tasted at a warmer temperature than they would be drunk socially. Medium and full-bodied reds are best at room temperature.

Red wines should be allowed to 'breathe' if possible before drinking. This is not necessary for white wines; they can be tasted straight away. But for most good quality reds it is important that the wine comes into contact with the air, because the oxygen interacts with the wine and brings out the flavours more fully. The most thorough way of achieving this is to decant the wine, which means to pour it into another container. This ensures that all of the wine has a chance to come into contact with the air. Second best is simply to open the bottle several hours before serving, but this only allows the wine at the top of the bottle to 'breathe'. In either case, many full-bodied reds benefit from being opened as much as 24 hours before drinking. Frequently a bottle left only half-drunk the previous evening will taste much better the next day. Try it out.

Just What Are You Tasting?

Most professional wine tasters will assess the wines 'blind' — that is, without knowing what they are tasting. The bottles are covered in foil or paper so that the wine is hidden from view and can be judged on its merits. This is a good method, as all tasters, professional or amateur, will invariably be influenced by knowing what the wine is before they taste. The first assessment to make is the colour of the wine, the second the smell, and lastly the taste.

SCORING WINES

There are a number of ways of scoring wine in tastings. The purpose of this is to allow comparison amongst wines, and to record the information for later recall. One of the easiest and most satisfactory is that shown in Figure 3.

Everyone tastes and scores differently, so one person's 9/20 may be another's 17/20. This is unimportant, as the purpose is to provide each individual with a memory bank of their own opinions. At a tasting of high quality organic wines attended by the buyers from several of the country's major retailers, a wine that one buyer thought was the worst in the room was independently applauded as probably the best by another. And thank goodness for that — if everyone had the same opinions we would face a miserably limited choice in the shops.

Colour

The colour of the wine should be judged by holding the glass against a white background, so that you are seeing it unaffected by other colours. The light needs to be good too. Hold the glass at an angle and look through the very top edge of the wine. You are checking that the wine is clear, bright, and pleasant to look at, and whether it has a pale or strong colour. It becomes immediately apparent that there is a huge range of colours and shades of white wine, from almost colourless wines to those with a richly golden hue. For reds the stage of development of the wine can be determined. When a wine is young it is a very purpley red; as it ages it will become gradually more towards brick red, and then on towards brown at the end of its life. When you have evolved some experience of tasting, identifying the stage of life of the wine in this way will give you a good idea of the taste even before the wine is in your mouth.

Bouquet

The smell is usually called the bouquet, or 'nose' in winespeak. If someone asks what it is like 'on the nose', they simply mean 'What does it smell like?' The bouquet of the wine is the key to knowing what it is. When very experienced pundits on television programmes are given a wine 'blind' and asked to identify it, and they get it right, this is largely because they have developed a huge memory bank of the smells of different wines. Some journalists are now staggeringly accurate at identifying wines in this way.

DATE: **VENUE:**   **SUBJECT:**

WINE	APPEARANCE	SMELL	TASTE	OVERALL ASSESSMENT	T O T A L
MUSCADET DE SEVRE ET MAINE SUR LIE 1989, DOMAINE DE LA PARENTIERE	Firm, greenish hue — some bubbles from the 'Petillance' 3	Lightly floral, citrus background. Slightly yeasty. 3	Good balance, high acidity offset by ample fruit flavour. Long finish 7	Very good quality muscadet 3	16
GEWURZ-TRAMINER 1989, PIERRE FRICK NON-CHAPTALIZED	Rich golden colour — marvellous, clear and bright 3	spicy, pungent, rich 4	Tremendously powerful, rich, almost oily. Fine length. 8	Superbly made, well rounded. Very typical 3	18
MULLER-THURGAU QbA, 1989, DIETMAR WERNER	Pale green, clear and correct 2	Ripe grape flavours, very upfront fresh and fruity. Appealing. 3	Good balance between the grapey flavour and background acidity 6	Well made again — good value for everyday 2	13
VIN DE PAYS DES MARCHES DE BRETAGNE, CEPAGE CABERNET, GUY BOSSARD	Purple red — very young but full 3	Lovely jammy fresh fruit bouquet — makes you want to hurry on to the taste! 3	Made to drink young and ripe, chewy, rich fruit red. Could be drunk chilled in summer? 7	Very appealing — no one would dislike it. Cleverly made. 2	15
HUNGARIAN ZWIEGELT 1989	Clear, clear and correct but a bit limp looking 2	Slightly off centre — fruity but rather unpleasant rubbery smell 1	Tasted on other occasions and much better - this is nasty, burnt, lacking in life and fruit. An off bottle or bad cuvée 2	Nothing like I remember — something wrong — poor. 0	5
DOMAINE RICHEAUME CABERNET SAUVIGNON COTES DE PROVENCE 1988	Full, dark purple — looks intriguing! 3	Classically blackcurrant flavour — wild and rich 3	Good tannin, still a bit young and coarse but great intensity of flavours — big, rich, weighty. 7	Hefty, well made — bags of character 3	16
SCORING	MAXIMUM 4	MAXIMUM 4	MAXIMUM 9	MAXIMUM 3	MAX 20

Fig 3: Tasting sheet

To each individual, wine smells and tastes different, and the catalogue of adjectives used to describe wines is an attempt to bridge this gap. However, some wines, or grapes, have clear and readily definable associations that just about everybody experiences in the same way. Amongst the most well known are the Gamay grape in Beaujolais which smells of boiled sweets; classic Sauvignon which smells of grass or cat's urine; dry Gewürztraminer which is very spicy and aromatic; and the red Cabernet Sauvignon which often smells strongly of blackcurrants. The Syrah grape of the south of France (the same as the Shiraz in Australia) often makes truly fabulous deep reds but on some occasions can produce wines with the smell of cowpats in a blocked drain! When tasting, try to avoid cigarette smoke, bonfires, kitchens with the dinner being cooked or any other strong smell which could affect the bouquet.

HOW TO TASTE

There is a huge difference between drinking wine and tasting it. If you simply drink wine as you might water or lemonade, you do not taste it. Why? Because our taste buds are not in our stomach. They are at the back of the mouth, and unless the wine is kept in the mouth for a decent amount of time, the full flavour will not be registered and transmitted to the brain for interpretation.

The way to taste a wine to its fullest is to take a sip into the mouth at the same time as inhaling a small amount of air. If you cannot manage this simultaneously, take the wine first and then suck in the air, rather like reverse whistling. Keeping wine and air in your mouth, first swirl it around, then chew the lot as though it were permanently-expanding candy floss. Concentrate on the flavours and sensations it provokes. Roll it around with your tongue so that all the taste buds get a fair crack. Once you have exhausted this process, either swallow it, or spit it into a spittoon or bucket. Professional wine tasters spit out wines after tasting simply because they would soon get drunk if they did not. Using this tasting technique for the first time, it is almost impossible not to feel a complete idiot and you are quite likely to cough and splutter. Do not be deterred! You will immediately have a much fuller taste of the wines, and this will quickly compensate for feelings of foolishness. And you can always practise spitting at home!

The key factor in all wines, whether dry or sweet, light or full-bodied, is the 'balance' or 'structure'. A good wine will have an equilibrium of its own, incorporating all the important characteristics of acidity, fruit, tannin and alcohol content. It will also be judged for its 'length'. This refers to the length of time the taste lingers in the mouth or throat. You can taste some wines which, once drunk or spat out, do not leave a lingering flavour. At the other extreme, a powerful flavour may remain for a considerable time. Generally, the longer the length of flavour, the better the wine.

The final judgement is whether all these factors add up to something pleasant. For the professional the task is not simply whether they personally like or dislike the wine, but if it is a good or bad example of a wine of its type.

To Be Remembered

'Cleaning the palate', which means allowing your taste buds to recover from one particular taste before tackling the next, is best done with plain dry bread or dry unsweetened biscuits. Water helps to refresh the mouth after tannic wines. A final word — do not eat strongly flavoured food such as garlic bread just before starting a tasting session! It would be a waste of wine!

SERVING WINE WITH FOOD

The main things to remember are temperature and the order in which wines are served. Make sure the wines are served at a temperature which will show each one at its best. Usually white and rosé wines are served chilled and red wines at room temperature. As a general guide, try full-bodied reds at around 16—18°C and dry whites at around 8°C.

Place them in the order which allows you to start with a dry sparkling wine or sherry before going on to a meal which progresses through dry white to light red, full-bodied red and finally sweet white with the dessert.

Always take off all of the foil capsule which is over the top of the cork and bottle, normally made of lead, and wipe the top of the bottle so that you pour wine, and not wine and lead traces, into the glass. You can reckon on 6 glasses per 75cl bottle. Be sure to have sufficient! If you are in a hurry and the whites are not cold enough, put them in the freezer. You would not be the first to put a red that needed warming into the microwave, although this is not recommended. When you buy wine in a restaurant and they offer a small glass to someone (almost invariably male, as though something in a male's genetic make-up makes him an inherently better judge than a female!), this is not to see if you like the wine. It is simply to check that the wine is as it should be — that it has not gone 'off'. One restaurant owner was enraged to discover after his day off that a new member of staff had opened 6 different bottles for one customer who seemed to think he could keep on trying wines until he found the one he liked the most!

Wine and Food

Large numbers of people live in fear of being exposed by their lack of knowledge of wines. Asked to select a bottle of wine to drink with a meal they will often dive for cover. How many times have you heard someone say stonefacedly 'I'm afraid I don't know much about wine'? Rightly or wrongly, being able to hold your own in a conversation about the relative merits of different wines carries social Brownie points, all the more so if you can select wines to go with food. But there is really no 'correct' combination of food and wine. There is only personal preference, and the accumulated wisdom of thousands or millions of people's preferences which lead us to suggested combinations. Wine and food combine well, either when they complement each other, or when they contrast. A sweet food with a sweet wine; or an oily smoked salmon with a crisp, highly acid Loire white wine. To give a general guide is very difficult, because it is ultimately a matter of each to his or her own taste. If you enjoy very expensive claret with fish and chips, then go ahead and do not be intimidated!

In any case, half the time people aren't sure what they're drinking. Try blindfolding your friends and sit them around the table. Explain that you are about to give them three glasses of wine in rotation. They have to taste each in turn, without being able to see it and judge whether it is red, white or rosé. You, as controller, have complete freedom over the choice of wines. Generally about 70 per cent are accurate on this 'blind' tasting. This means that nearly one in three people cannot tell the colour of the wine they are drinking without seeing it. Next introduce various different foods, also while your friends are blindfolded, and ask them to taste each food with each of the wines to assess compatibility. If all goes according to the received wisdom, they will not like the dry Muscadet with the chocolate but will enjoy the heavy Port with the richly flavoured Stilton. Do they, in fact?

As a rule, dry and medium white wines go well with seafood dishes, white meats, light or vegetarian foods; heavy, full-bodied sweet white wines with rich desserts; light red wines with salmon, lighter red meats, or white bean dishes; full-bodied and powerful red wines with strongly-flavoured meat dishes, red bean dishes, and strong cheese. Some foods, such as spicy Indian or ice cream, really do not go with wine at all. But just about every wine can be paired with a food. The ultimate purpose of matching wine with food is to make each one taste better when linked to the other than they would be if consumed separately.

The last thing to say about wine is — enjoy it. Pierre Barron, producer of the organic Château Meric, in the Graves region south of Bordeaux, says 'Drink a little but drink well; drink naturally so that you can drink for a long time'.

This encapsulates the right approach. In restricted amounts, drinking wine can enhance physical and mental well-being. The recommended maximum alcohol intake is 3 glasses of wine a day for men and 2 for women, preferably with food and including some days without a drink. Excessive alcohol consumption is clearly bad. Excessive consumption of sulphur dioxide, chemical additives and pesticide residues is not likely to improve the body either. 'You are what you drink' is just as true as 'you are what you eat'. Today's message is to watch the alcohol and, when you do drink, drink organic.

PART TWO

6

WINE LISTINGS

In the following pages we describe some 500 organic drinks on sale in the UK. Each entry is accompanied by a series of codes and a description of its qualities.

In some cases the information on which the codes were based was not available. This is most frequent in regard to whether the wine is suitable for vegetarians or vegans. In such cases the code has been replaced with a question mark.

All the information presented was checked at the time of writing, but prices and vintages can change without warning, and some wines may no longer be available. We apologize for any inconvenience this may cause. All French wines are AC, Appellation Contrôlée, quality unless otherwise indicated.

We have tasted most, but not all, of the wines listed and it has to be accepted that this is very much a personal view. We have attempted to remain objective, but it must be recognized that everyone tastes things differently. Please taste the wines and compare your own judgement with ours (and let us know what you think by returning the readers' comments page at the back of the book).

READING THE CODES

The line of codes immediately under the name of the wine consists of (in this order) the keeping quality or when best to drink; the sweetness or weight indicator; the price guide; the organic verification; and the suitability of the wine for vegetarians and vegans. The codes following the description refer to the UK wholesaler and high street stockist.

Example

Guy Bossard, Muscadet de Sèvre et Maine sur Lie, 1989
1 £b FESA VE

Accolades time again as far as this wine is concerned. Ever since Guy Bossard's 1986 came out top in a Muscadet tasting run by *Which Wine Monthly,* this wine has been praised in the press . . .
VRT; VIN; HDR; WHI; OWC; ASD

when to drink:
sweetness: 1;
price: b;
organic organization: FESA;
suitability for vegetarians and vegans: VE;
suppliers: VRT, VIN, HDR, WHI, OWC, ASD.

WHEN TO DRINK

= Drink now.

= Should improve if kept but also fine to drink now.

= Needs keeping before drinking.

= Fully matured and won't improve at all with keeping.

SWEETNESS OR WEIGHT INDICATOR

White and rosé wines, champagnes and some fortified wines are graded on a scale from 1—9. 1 indicates the driest style such as a Muscadet, Champagne or Sancerre; 9 the sweetest as in certain of the top quality German wines.

Red wines are graded on a scale from A—E. A is the lightest style, usually a Vin de Table; E the most full-bodied as in an Italian Barolo.

This coding is not applicable to brandies or beers, hence the notation N/A.

This grading is based on that of the Wine Development Board's classification. A leaflet on the subject can be obtained from their headquarters at Five Kings House, 1 Queen Street Place, London EC4R 1QS. This is reproduced in Appendix 1.

PRICE

Most of the wines listed are available by the case of 12 bottles from mail order companies or from the independent retailers they supply. The codes refer to the price of the bottle, including VAT, when bought by the case. Where wines are stocked by off-licence chains and supermarkets, the price is usually not too different from the mail order case price, so the code is a good guide.

Price (per bottle, including VAT)
£a = Under £2.99
£b = £3.00—£4.99
£c = £5.00—£6.99
£d = £7.00—£9.99
£e = £10.00—£14.99
£f = Over £15.00

ORGANIC VERIFICATION

The abbreviation for the organic organization that the winemaker belongs to is given. Where IND is stated for Independent, we have endeavoured to ensure that the producer is genuinely adhering to organic principles in both growing the vines and making the wine. In some cases this has been achieved through our own knowledge of the producer, supported by signed statements; but in most we have taken the information from the UK importer or retailer. Readers should be aware that Independent organic growers are not subject to the same external controls as those belonging to standards associations.

Listel

The huge Listel company in the south of France produces wines which are widely available in the UK and are often sold as organic wines, although the producers do not belong to any of the organic associations. They are a good example of the difficulties that surround the issue of 'independent' producers. The company is based in the Golfe du Lion in the Mediterranean, where the climate and sea sands enable them to produce wines without many chemical inputs. The wines are generally of good quality and they lay claim to using organic methods of production. While they certainly use very few chemical inputs, it is hard to discern from their literature if they actually guarantee not to use any. Nevertheless, it would appear that wines made exclusively from their own Golfe du Lion vineyards are as 'organic' as those of any other independent producer. However, they also produce products which are made partly from vines grown in the Golfe du Lion in their own vineyards, and partly from bought-in grapes which they make no claims about. Such wines include their widely-distributed 'Pétillant de Listel', a sparkling low alcohol wine which is often advertised by UK retailers as being organic. It is made without the use of SO_2, a major plus point, but it cannot be said that all the grapes are organically grown. A further complicating factor is that Listel also sell wines from vineyards in the Rhône about which no organic claims are made. It is worth noting that the company does not in general seek to promote its wines on the basis of their being organic, preferring rather to stress the quality of the products.

Organic Codes and their Full Names

France
BIOPLAMPAC = Association Inter-Régionale des Agrobiologistes du Quart Sud-Ouest de la France
D = Demeter (trademark of the Biodynamic Association)
DYN = Dynorga (trademark of biodynamic grower M Daumas and one or two of his associates)
EAP = Environnement—Alimentation—Progrès
FESA = Fédération Européenne des Syndicats d'Agrobiologistes
FNAB = Fédération Nationale de l'Agriculture Biologique
GA = Groupement d'Agrobiologistes
NP = Nature et Progrès
PAG = Paysan Agrobiologiste
UNIA = Union Nationale Interprofessionelle de l'Agrobiologie

Germany
ANOG = Arbeitsgemeinshaft für Naturnahen Obst-, Gemüse-, und Feldfruchtanbau
BIO = Bioland (also used on Italian wines)
BOW = Bundesverband Okologischer Weinbau
ROAWR = Ring Okologisch Arbeitender Winzer Rheinhessen

Italy
AIB = Associazione Italiana per l'Agricoltura Biologica
BIODYN = Biodyn (the conversion grade of Demeter)

BIO = Bioland (a German scheme — see above)
D = Demeter
SS = Suolo e Salute

Others
Spain: VS = Vida Sana
England: SA = Soil Association
Australia: NASAA = National Association for Sustainable Agriculture in Australia
USA: CCOF = California Certified Organic Growers
Hungary: EKO = Hungarian wines are certified by the Dutch group Stichting Ekomerk Control (SEC)
New Zealand: BIOGROW = New Zealand Biological Producers' Council
Portugal: AGROBIO = Associaçao Portugesa de Agricultura Biológica

VEGETARIAN AND VEGAN WINES

V = the wine is suitable for vegetarians
VE = the wine is suitable for vegetarians and vegans
No = the wine is not suitable for either vegans or vegetarians.

This categorization is based on whether or not any animal products were used in the process of making the wine, notably in the fining. If egg whites were used, for example, the wine would be suitable for vegetarians, but not for vegans who avoid all animal products. It is entirely possible, however, that some of those wines classified as being suitable for vegans may be derived from grapes fertilized with animal manures, as we were not always able to obtain such specific information from all the suppliers.

It should be noted that those fining agents which may be derived from animal products — such as casein or gelatine — are not usually present in the wine when bottled (except occasionally in minute traces) but pass through it and are then discarded.

SUPPLIERS

Importer/Wholesaler (see Chapter 9 for addresses and mail order details)
COW = A Case of Wine

DUN = Dunkertons Cider Co
GJF = Goujon and Fils Ltd
HDR = HDRA (Sales) Ltd
HFW = Haughton Fine Wines
ORG = Organics
OWC = The Organic Wine Company Ltd
ROD = Rodgers Fine Wines
SED = Sedlescombe Organic Wines
VIN = Vinceremos
VRT = Vintage Roots
WCL = Winecellars
WHI = Whitakers Wines

Off-licence and Wine Merchant Chains (see also Chapter 7, The High Street)
ABT = Augustus Barnett
BLA = Blayneys
BUP = Bottoms Up
MWW = Majestic Wine Warehouse
ODD = Oddbins
THR = Threshers
WRK = Wine Rack
WWW = Wizard Wine Warehouse

Supermarkets (see also Chapter 7, The High Street)
ASD = Asda
CRS = Co-op/Leos
EDB = Edwin Booth
SAF = Safeway
SAN = Sainsbury
TES = Tesco
WAI = Waitrose
WMO = William Morrisons

WHITE WINES

FRANCE

Alsace

Edelzwicker, Stentz, litre bottles
2 £c NP V

Edelzwicker is the term for blended wines in Alsace, of lower quality than the individual grape varieties. This litre bottle offers quaffable stuff for every day. Pale, light and dryish.
  OWC

Gewürztraminer, Steingrübler Grand Cru, Stentz 1987
4 £d NP V

The Steingrübler part of the name refers to the vineyard site where the grapes were grown, this being a *Cru* vineyard, meaning it produces consistently high quality wines. The wine is one that will develop for many years, although very good now. Higher in alcohol than the non-cru vineyards.
  OWC

Gewürztraminer, Pierre Frick 1988/9
4 £c D VE

Silver Medal International Wine Challenge 1990 (1988 vintage). A richly weighty, heady wine from the Frick family; both vintages have a fine rich colour and open, irresistible character. Medium-dry, spicy and flowery, the 1989 smells of roses and is a mighty 14 degrees of alcohol without chaptalization. Top notch stuff.
  HDR; VIN

Gewürztraminer, Meyer 1988
3 £c/d D VE

Although not produced on one of Meyer's Cru vineyards, his high standards and excellent quality are present in this wine. Medium-dry, rich and succulent.
HFW; COW; WHI

Gewürztraminer, Stentz 1987/89
3 £c/d NP V

Another of the many good Gewürztraminers from the organic growers of Alsace, a medium dry richly golden wine with an oily, spicy flavour.
VRT; OWC

Gewürztraminer Grand Cru Spiegel, Meyer 1986
4 £d D VE

Lovely perfumed, elegant bouquet, full of fresh Gewürz character. It tastes really clean and fresh with good balance and fine structure. A very well tailored wine, from another Cru vineyard. Not chaptalized.
HFW; WHI

Gewürztraminer, Steingrübler Vendanges Tardives, Stentz 1986
5 £e NP V

One of a clutch of truly delicious wines from the Alsatian organic trio of Stenz, Frick and Meyer. 'Vendanges tardives' means late harvested, the significance of which is that the grapes stay on the vines for longer than usual, achieving a higher sugar content. This does not necessarily make them sweeter — the vinification and preparation of the wine determines that — but they are more alcoholic. This is 14 degrees, with a comparable intensity of flavour.
OWC

Gewürztraminer Grand Cru Spiegel Vendanges Tardives, 1986, Meyer
5 £f D VE

The most noticeable aspect of this wine is the enormous length it has, that is, the quite extraordinary and impressive flavour lingering on and on long after you have swallowed the wine. Fabulous, elegant nose, soft, rich flavour. Not chaptalized.
HFW; WHI

Klevner-Pinot Blanc, Frick 1987/8
4 £c D VE

Described by *Elle* magazine in France as 'having a yellowy green colour, a bouquet of pineapples and the flowers of the vine, the wine is fresh, fruity, alive and supple'. And so it is. Made without chaptalization.
HDR; VIN

Klevner-Pinot Blanc, Meyer 1988
4 £c D VE

Clean appley taste, fresh and with a nice hint of acidity.
HFW; COW

Muscat d'Alsace, Meyer 1988
5 £c D VE

Gold Medal Winner, Colmar, Alsace. Sumptuous wine, magnificent perfumed Muscat bouquet followed by a crisp dry flavour. Drink it now or store for a few years and watch it evolve.
HFW; WHI

Riesling, Frick 1986/8
2 £c D VE

Fullish body and smooth, with a very pronounced complex flavour, rich, oily and concentrated. The most particularly distinctive feature of this vintage is the high acidity — the wine is positively cutting in its bite, while following up with the fullness of the fruit. High time for a Riesling revival with wines like this available. Not chaptalized.
HDR; VIN

Riesling, Meyer 1987
4 £c D VE

Considered to be the great grape of Alsace, well made Riesling can be a wonderful combination of opposites, light but at the same time powerful, firm but also flowery. It is often said to smell of oil or petrol, but this fine example is more floral. Dry, full-bodied and intriguing.
HFW; COW

Riesling, Stentz 1988
2 £c NP V

Green to gold colour, slightly spiky bouquet, restrained grape character.
OWC

Sylvaner, Frick 1986/8
3 £b D VE

A delightful wine that trips off the tongue, lightish, creamy, mellow and full of soft fruit. Fairly straightforward style. The grape variety is often regarded as a bit average in the UK, but this example is a fine appealing wine. It has a well balanced golden/yellow colour and very accessible fruity character. Almost tailor-made for those who like dry but not bitingly sharp wines. Not chaptalized.
HDR; VIN

Sylvaner, Meyer 1988
3 £c D VE

Gold Medal Winner, Colmar. Simply excellent. The straightforward flavour and pleasant grape bouquet makes this an easy and friendly wine. Lighter in body than the Gewürztraminers and Rieslings, and with slightly more acidity than some. It doesn't command your attention in quite the same way as the others: sometimes a welcome relief!
HFW; COW; WHI

Tokay d'Alsace, Stentz 1988
3 £c NP V

From the Pinot Gris grape, spicy and dry in style with a rich buttery character.
VRT; OWC

Tokay d'Alsace, Meyer 1988
4 £d D VE

Gold Medal Winner, Colmar. We tasted this wine with Madame Meyer in Alsace, offered to us as evidence of the generally high standards her wines attain. A very rich, fat, rounded flavour with a strong, almost bitter aftertaste. Good structure, an excellent, well made wine fully deserving of her pride.
HFW; COW; WHI

Tokay Pinot Gris, Steingrübler Vendanges Tardives, Stentz 1986
4 £e NP ?

This Vendange Tardive wine is generally more concentrated in flavour, bouquet and colour than the wine from grapes picked earlier, and just a little sweeter. More expensive because more grapes go into producing each bottle, and there is extra work involved.
OWC

Bordeaux

Domaine du Grand Loup, Blayais 1989
1 £a FESA VE

From the region north of Bordeaux on the right bank of the famous Gironde, where the Garonne and Dordogne rivers meet. The area also produces decent value-for-money reds. This white has become very popular and is one of the best value dry white organic wines available at the lower end of the price range. From Ugni Blanc grapes, it is well made, with interesting melony character and a bit of zip in the finish.
VRT

Domaine de Jullouc, Côtes de Blaye 1987
1 £b FESA VE

Colombard grapes here make an interesting well-rounded wine, plenty of interacting flavours, surprisingly concentrated. Another good value wine within the general style.
VRT

Château Balluemondon, Bordeaux 1989
1 £b FESA VE

Predominantly Semillon, with some Sauvignon and Muscadelle, this is a slightly flatter-tasting vintage than normal. The Semillon character predominates in the 1989, whereas the 1988 had a livelier, zesty fruit character. The 1990 is awaited with interest.
VIN; HDR

Château Balluemondon, Bordeaux Moelleux 1988/90
6 £b FESA VE

A delicious medium sweet white, the same wine as the dry from this estate, but from later-picked grapes with more residual sugar. The sweetness is beautifully integrated in the body of the wine, making this a splendid aperitif.
HDR; VIN

Château Busqueyron, Bordeaux Sec 1987/88
1 £b UNIA V

Jean-Marc Maugey has taken over the property from his father René and is experimenting with biodynamic methods. If our visit to the estate was anything to go by, this decision does nothing to enhance harmony between the generations! A fairly unconventional wine

that is likely to produce strong reactions. The rather idiosyncratic style has led to it being de-classified as an Entre-Deux-Mers; it is now sold simply as Bordeaux Blanc. While the wine has the nice fruit of pears in the bouquet when young and fresh, it has a rather waxy and strong, almost bitter flavour. From about 70 per cent Semillon and a blend of Sauvignon, Muscadelle and Ugni Blanc.
VRT

Château la Chapelle Maillard, Bordeaux 1989
1 £b NP VE

Excellent crisp dry white, probably the best vintage yet from Jean-Luc and Renée Devert, on their small 8-hectare vineyard near St Quentin de Caplong, 25 kilometres from St Emilion. The wine is from the usual white Bordeaux blend and has lovely acidity producing excellent freshness and fruit. Sometimes the predominance of the Semillon grape can make white Bordeaux a little heavy, possibly even dull. This has bags of life. Bronze Medal, Concours Générale Paris 1990.
HDR; VIN

Château le Gorre, Bordeaux, 1989/90
1 £b FESA No

From 50 per cent each Sauvignon and Semillon, with the colour of the Semillon and the nose of the Sauvignon. Clean, well balanced and carefully made. Very good example of well-crafted white Bordeaux.
HFW

Château des Hautes Combes, Bordeaux Sec Sauvignon 1989/90
1 £b FESA VE

Again, best consumed when young to benefit from the fruit at its freshest. A zippy, nicely dry wine, good fruit, pale in colour. 100 per cent Sauvignon grapes.
VRT; OWC; VIN; HDR

Château Le Maubastit, Bordeaux Sec 1989
1 £b FESA ?

Pale in colour, a straightforward wine, direct and uncomplicated. Fairly typical basic white Bordeaux.
OWC

Château Moulin de Romage, Bordeaux Sec 1989
1 £b NP VE

Light, crisp white best drunk early to capture the freshness of the flavour.
VRT; ORG

Château Moulin de Romage, Bordeaux Supérieur, Moelleux 1989
7 £b NP VE

'Moelleux' means mellow, and this sweet white lives up to the name. Made from late-picked Semillon grapes, it has depth of body to partner the cool sweetness; this is more an aperitif style than a dessert wine, being rich but not heavily sweet.
VIN; HDR; VRT; HFW; COW; OWC

Château Haut Mallet, Bordeaux Haut Benage 1989
4 £c FNAB V

Sauvignon, Semillon, Muscadelle, a forthright yellow green colour and positive, robust flavour. Fine, soft lengthy finish.
HFW; WHI

Château Canet, Entre-Deux-Mers 1989/90
1 £b IND VE

Crisp and fresh with nice balance of acidity and fruit. Full, grapey bouquet (pear drops) and deliciously juicy in the mouth. Well-made wine from a blend of Semillon and Sauvignon grapes. The 1990 vintage has extraordinary weight and presence, with exceptional length of flavour, carrying unusually high alcohol content.
SAF

Château Vieux-Gabiran, Entre-Deux-Mers 1990
1 £b NP VE

High scores generally in the Entre-Deux-Mers category — the region (literally meaning 'Between Two Seas', which are actually the two rivers of the Garonne and Dordogne) can produce both nice fruity whites and rather boring flat wines. This has an excellent fruit bouquet and rounded rich flavour. Friendly and open are the adjectives that spring to mind. Very well made, it captures the spirit of the wine.
VIN; HDR; VRT

Château Large-Malartic, Entre-Deux-Mers 1989
1 £b IND VE
A crisp, dry fruity white. It has a light juicy bouquet with lovely fresh taste in the mouth. Well made.
WWW

Château La Croix Simon, Entre-Deux-Mers, 1988/9
1 £b NP V
Upfront pear drops is the immediate smell, backed up by a solid firm flavour. A well-made all-round example in typical Entre-Deux-Mers style, not overly dry. A wine that will accompany most light foods.
OWC

Domaine Bourdieu, Entre-Deux-Mers, 1989
2 £b FNAB V
From Sauvignon, Semillon and Muscadelle, the grassy Sauvignon stands out in the bouquet and the light fruitiness carries through into the flavour. Fresh and juicy, best to drink young.
HFW; COW; WHI

Château Meric Graves 1989
1 £b NP VE
This is a little like a very high quality Entre-Deux-Mers; it has pears in the bouquet with a wonderfully succulent ripe mouthful to follow. Firm background weight.
HDR; VIN; ASD

Clos La Maurasse, Graves 1987/8
2 £c UNIA V
Half each Sauvignon and Semillon, pale yellow in colour with quite a strong floral bouquet. The flavour fills the mouth; we'd like to taste later vintages too.
HFW(88); COW(87)

Clos de la Perichère, Graves Supérieur 1986
1 £c UNIA V
Pale in colour, the wine needs drinking. This is really getting past its best at this stage. The estate is generally a producer of high quality wines, so the younger vintages should be good.
WHI

Château St Hilaire, Graves Supérieur 1982
1 £c UNIA V

This top-quality estate produces marvellous reds, and the white is
no disappointment. Really quite old for this type of dry white, the
usual fashion nowadays being to make them fresh and young. We
tasted the wine some time ago when it was round and firm in the
mouth, quite buttery and with a good long finish. Definitely a wine
of class, but it's likely to be tiring by now. Try later vintages if you
can.
WHI

Burgundy

Bourgogne Aligoté, Domaine Musso 1988
2 £c NP ?

Aged in new oak barrels, Aligoté is the 'other' white wine grape of
Burgundy. While it generally lacks the round rich softness of good
Chardonnay, it gains in bite and crispness. This is a fine example,
clean with nice acid content. Direct in its appeal.
HFW

Bourgogne Blanc, A Chaumont 1986
3 £c UNIA V

Another appealing Chardonnay with nicely integrated fruit
flavours, dry but not biting. The fruit flavour comes through well.
HFW

Bourgogne Blanc, Alain Guillot 1988
2 £c FNAB VE

Chardonnay from one of the most orthodox of all organic growers.
Wax over the top of the bottle gives added protection against the
air. From the Mâcon region, the wine is for early drinking. Good
golden hue, an easy, inviting wine.
WHI

Côte de Beaune Blanc, Domaine E Giboulet 1986
2 £d NP VE

From a single hectare of vines, with a low yield at 25—30 hectolitres
per year. The produce of 'vielles vignes' — the old vines which tend
to give lower yields and more concentrated fruit flavour. Aged in
new oak for 14—16 months, this is really classy stuff, yellow colour
and fine flavour. Watch out also for the 1988 vintage, tasted in

France and found to be full, fat and rounded, a strong and characterful wine of top quality.
COW

Côte de Beaune, La Grande Châtelaine 1987/88
2 £d NP VE

Bronze Medal Winner International Wine Challenge 1989. Subtle, soft Chardonnay, dry but level, with a recognizable Chardonnay bouquet of toasty biscuits. A delicate variety of flavours. Dignified stuff from the Chardonnay grape.
VRT

Givry, Guy Chaumont 1987
2 £c/d NP VE

Pale colour with a slightly green hue. Buttery flavour, stronger in taste than the colour implies. Chardonnay grapes producing a good value, subtle and delicate wine.
HDR; VIN; VRT

Hautes Côtes de Nuits Chardonnay, A. Verdet 1987
3 £d FNAB V

Chardonnay again, nice golden colour, full and rich in the mouth. Citrus overtones, tangy finish — leaves you with the impression of finely crafted excellence.
HDR; HFW; OWC; VIN; VRT; WHI

Meursault Jean Javillier 1988
2 £d/e NP V

With sufficient pedigree to improve further in the bottle, a full, rich wine with a creamy flavour and the overall feel of quality.
VRT; OWC

Puligny Montrachet, Rateau 1988/9
2 £e NP ?

A producer who is organic and uses biodynamic methods. Puligny-Montrachet is one of the villages in the Beaune area of Burgundy, capable of producing top flight wines. Pierrette and Jean-Claude Rateau do just that. The rich, buttery, initial flavour supported by nicely weighted acidity make this outstanding.
VRT

Bourgogne Aligoté, Alain Verdet, 1989
1 £c FNAB V

Clean fresh flavour, more body than most Aligoté, quite buttery and with good definition to the wine. Good acidity, direct and with an almost waxy background flavour.
OWC; WHI

Jura

Côtes du Jura 1986
2 £c FESA V

Michel Terrier's whites are from the Chardonnay grape for the usual wine, which is dry and fruity, and from Chardonnay and Savagnin (yes, not Sauvignon) for the Cuvée Réserve. The Réserve is fuller and more rounded. Both are aged in oak prior to bottling and have the very distinctive Jura style which has close associations with the style of dry sherry.
WHI

Languedoc-Roussillon

Chardonnay, Vin de Pays de l'Aude 1989
2 £b UNIA No

Reminiscent of some of the best Chardonnays from Northern Italy, the wine is delightfully fragrant, succulent and fruity. This is one of those wines that it would be hard for anyone to dislike; with a nice youthful green colour, its hallmark is being balanced and well-rounded, not too dry. It is not marked as vegetarian or vegan because the producer reserves the right to use isinglass if necessary when fining the wine. This, he says, produces a greater sheen to the brightness of the colour than do the other clarifying agents.
HDR; VIN

Château de Caraguilhes, Blanc de Blancs Corbières, 1989
3 £b UNIA V

100 per cent Grenache Blanc, available in what are known as 'serigraphiées' bottles, where the paper label is replaced by an imprint in the glass of the bottle. Yellow straw colour and aromatic nose, nicely acidic with a hint of liquorice. An excellent example of how to achieve balance in a wine.
HFW; COW

Château Caderonne, Limoux, 1989
1 £b UNIA VE

From one small estate just south of the town of Limoux, a rare opportunity to taste a still wine from this area. Most production is geared towards the famous sparkling wine, Blanquette de Limoux (see the section on sparkling wines for two organic examples). This dry white is made from the Mauzac grape and has a very thick yellow colour and slightly waxy texture. Strongly perfumed and flavoured with a slightly bitter, nutty character, derived from the Mauzac grape. A distinctive and individual style of wine.

HDR; VIN; BUP

Côtes du Roussillon, Blanc de Blancs Coronat
2 £b NP V

Silver Medal winner at the Concours Générale de Paris in 1988. Crisp, lively wine, light and delicate. From Muscat grapes, vinified as a dry wine and producing a flavour quite typical of the grape.

VRT

Domaine de Mayrac, Vin de Pays de l'Aude 1989
2 £b NP V

Light green in colour, from the Mauzac grape, we have tasted this wine on many occasions over the past year and it has increasingly impressed us. Initially it seemed a little bland, but it is nicely balanced, clean, friendly and pleasantly green. An ideal wine for everyday drinking.

VRT; HDR; VIN

Domaine de Mayrac Chardonnay, Vin de Pays D'Oc, 1989
2 £b NP V

The labels on this wine look as though they have gone rusty; apparently it's a nimble piece of design work, somewhat 'à la mode'. The wine is much better than the label, no hint of metal, and just a touch of the crusty, yeasty character of good Chardonnay. Dry and accessible, a decent mouthful.

VRT; HDR; VIN

Domaine de Petit Roubié, Vin de Pays des Côtes de Thau, 1989
3 £b NP V

This is a wine we just cannot like. It has a flat, burnt flavour, lacking in acidity and without freshness or life. This is what lots of whites from the Midi taste like, and maybe some people like this style, but it's got about as much interest as a mid-term party political broadcast!

HFW; VIN; HDR

Domaine de Villeroy-Castellas, Vin de Pays des Sables du Golfe du Lion, 1988/9
1 £b IND VE

100 per cent Sauvignon grapes, a wine made for early drinking. Light, fresh fruit flavour and good balance — not overly acidic nor bland and dull, as can easily happen with southern whites. Well made.

ABT; EDB

Vin de Pays Catalan Muscat Sec, Clos St Martin 1989
3 £b NP ?

100 per cent Muscat, pale yellow colour with a light grapey nose. Soft, fruity, dry style.

HFW

Vin de Pays de Charentais, Brard Blanchard 1988
2 £b NP ?

Fresh flowers predominate in the bouquet. Pale yellow in colour. Winner of a Silver medal at the Paris Concours Générale, a light and refreshing wine from the Ugni Blanc grape. An example of the increasing number of good dry whites being made in the area that is best known for producing cognac.

HFW; OWC

Limoux, 1989
2 £b UNIA V

From the town famous for the sparkling Blanquette de Limoux, this still wine is dry and ripe. Made from the Mauzac grape, which can give quite a strong, nutty flavour, this character is only just perceptible here. Almost sherbety in taste, with a nice light green colour. Delightfully succulent.

HDR; VIN

Mauzac, Vin de Pays de l'Aude 1989
1 £b UNIA No

From the same estate that produces the Chardonnay (page 95), this has a vibrant green colour and richly nutty taste. The Mauzac grape is hardly used outside this region. More of this type of 'high juice' Vin de Pays style would be welcome. An ideal everyday wine.

VRT; HDR; VIN

Loire

Blanc de Blancs, Guy Bossard
1 £b FESA VE

Third in the hierarchy of Guy's white wines, after the Muscadet and Gros Plant, the Blanc de Blancs is a blend of Gros Plant and Muscadet young vines — those that are producing fruit but are not yet appropriate for Appellation Contrôlée and VDQS status. It is softer than the Gros Plant, has a bit more edge to it than the Muscadet, but is very clearly from the same exceptional pedigree — dry, zesty, lemony, tangy and bursting with life.

VRT; HDR; VIN; EDB

Gros Plant du Pays Nantais sur Lie, Guy Bossard, VDQS, 1988
1 £b FESA VE

The unattractive sounding Gros Plant (pronounced Grow Plon) grape is best known for producing Loire valley whites that are so dry and acidic they make a mouthful of raw cooking apples seem soft and mellow. It is a grape of little renown. However this need not necessarily be the case and when made well, as here, it shows just what a difference good fruit and high quality wine making can make. Better than most Muscadet, Bossard's Gros Plant is bone-dry but not overly acidic; it has a terrific zing, nice fruit to balance things out, and an overall character of citrus. Made 'sur Lie', which means keeping the wine on the yeast deposits rather than racking it off, it has a pleasant 'pétillance' or sparkle.

VIN; HDR; WHI; OWC; WAI (according to availability)

**Domaine de la Parentière, VDQS, Gros Plant du Pays Nantais
sur Lie 1988/89**
1 £b NP V

From Michel and Odile Menager's small estate, one of only two
organic Gros Plants in existence, this is made 'sur Lie' like their
Muscadet and is lightly spritzy as a result. Very dry, but crisply
fruity, plenty of bite and ideal for hot weather drinking.
VRT

Muscadet de Sèvre et Maine sur Lie, Guy Bossard, 1989
1 £b FESA VE

Accolades time again, as far as this wine is concerned. Ever since
Guy Bossard's 1986 came out top in a Muscadet tasting, run by
Which? Wine Monthly, this wine has been praised in the press,
vintage after vintage. And rightly so, for it is consistently one of the
very best Muscadets produced. Its undoubted quality has been one
of the major influences in establishing the credibility of organic
wine making among UK wine buyers. It is from the Muscadet
heartland — the Sèvre et Maine — where the best quality wines are
to be found. Added to this is its 'sur Lie' nature which gives the
wine a slight sparkle. The 1989 vintage won a Bronze medal (only)
at the 1990 International Wine Challenge. *Which? Wine Monthly*
said of the earlier vintage 'If only all Muscadet tasted like this!'; the
Independent called the 1989 'ripe, lemony, with a salty tang and a
prickle of fizz'. It is a delightfully fruity, fresh, dry wine, low in SO_2.
VRT; VIN; HDR; WHI; OWC; ASD

**Domaine de la Parentière, Muscadet de Sèvre et Maine sur Lie
1989/90**
1 £b NP VE

Not far from Guy Bossard's estate is the smaller property of Michel
and Odile Menager. This is the only other verified organic
Muscadet available, and it maintains the proof of how good organic
wines can be. The Menagers always use the traditionally-shaped
bottle of the region, which reminds us of a swan in flight — long-
necked but quite bulbous in the body. Also an excellent wine, it
perhaps comes just below Guy Bossard's in the pecking order, but
is also very delicious. Nice balance of acidity and fruit, good zesty
mouthful. Just what good Muscadet should be like.
VRT; VIN; HDR; CRS; WRK

Muscadet de Sèvre et Maine sur Lie 'Hermine d'Or' Guy Bossard
1987/8
🍾 1 £b/c FESA VE
Every year top Muscadet producers in the Loire submit their special
Cuvée wines for the award of the Hermine d'Or. This award, given
by the local wine committee, is restricted to the very best wines.
Guy Bossard's wines seem to be selected for just about every
vintage. The wines chosen have a fuller, richer, weightier character
than the Muscadet for immediate drinking, and they have the
potential to develop in the bottle for several years. The 1988 is now
drinking well and will continue to develop for some time; the 1987,
which has a yeasty, musty character typical of some vintages, is
unlikely to improve further.
    VRT; VIN; HDR; WHI; OWC

🍾 *Christian Dauny, Sancerre 1989*
🍷 1 £c/d FESA V
100 per cent Sauvignon grape. The importer's descriptive notes
refer to this as 'A white wine whose floral fragrance is marked by a
dominant marigold and some blackcurrant', and recommend that
it be drunk when accompanying a goat cheese such as 'Crottin de
Chavignol' from the Sancerre region. If only we could! Earlier
vintages were a bit lacklustre but this is delightful, lots of vibrant
grassy flavour, a generally succulent mouthful with nice balance.
Best during the year after bottling while the freshness of the fruit
is still predominant.
    VRT; VIN; HDR; OWC; GJF

🍾 *Domaine du Mont-Poirrier, Sauvignon de Touraine 1989*
🍷 1 £b NP VE
From the Touraine region of the Loire, another excellent
Sauvignon. A full flavoured bouquet (do we detect gooseberries
and elderflower?), and luscious rounded mouthful.
    VRT

🍾 *Domaine Didier Pabiot, Pouilly-Fumé 1989*
🍷 4 £d IND ?
From a small vineyard of just 4 hectares, Didier Pabiot produces a
lovely rich fruity wine. The overall impression is one of wealth —
of flavour, bouquet and colour. Delicious.
    HFW

Domaine de Dreuille, Coteaux du Layon 1988/89
7 £b EAP VE

The Coteaux du Layon is an Appellation Contrôlée area in the Anjou region of the Loire valley. Its wines are delightfully sweet without being hard work. From the Chenin Blanc grape, this example is smooth and velvety. The wines age well, becoming more concentrated in flavour and darker in colour as time passes. Do not be alarmed to find the sugar crystallizing in the bottom of the bottle. Equally, they make good, fruitier wines when drunk young. Higher in SO_2 than dry wines because of the increased danger of oxidation caused by the higher sugar level.

ORG; VRT

Coteaux du Layon, Gérard Leroux 1973
7 £c NP VE

The older they get, the sweeter they get. There are not too many old vintages commercially available from the small amounts normally produced by organic growers, so this is a bit of a treasure. The sweetness is more concentrated now, but it is not sickly sweet, and the wine makes a lovely dessert or after dinner drink. Rich golden colour. Chenin Blanc grapes, with a harmless natural deposit in the bottles.

VIN; HDR

Coteaux du Layon, Gérard Leroux 1986/7
8 £b NP V

Very similar in style to the older 1973, higher in acidity and not as mature. Nice glycerine, fat style of wine, excellent now as an aperitif or keep for years and serve as an 'end of the meal' drink.

VIN; HDR; WHI(1987 only); HFW(1986 only)

Domaine de Dreuillé, Anjou Sec 1989
1 £b EAP VE

Crisply dry as one would expect from an Anjou Chenin Blanc. A background of citrus fruit flavours.

VRT

Provence

Château Barbeyrolles, Blanc de Blancs Côtes de Provence 1988
2 £d IND ?

Ugni Blanc, Rolle and Semillon grapes, pale yellow colour, firm clean fruit charcater.

HFW

*Château la Tour de l'Evêque, Blanc de Blancs Côtes de Provence
1988*
3 £c IND ?

This estate is owned by Régine and Roger Sumeire who also own
Château Barbeyrolles nearby. The wines are of very similar style
from the two properties: here also Ugni Blanc, Rolle and Semillon,
with some Clairette. Light yellow colour and full smokey flavour.
HFW

Domaine du Jas d'Esclans, Cru Classé Côtes de Provence 1989
2 £b IND V

The regional Ugni Blanc, Clairette and Rolle pop up again. Lemony
overtones to this one, not too dry. Capture it young while the
freshness and fruit last. This estate produces wines in both the
conventional Bordeaux-shaped bottles and or the very long, coca-
cola style that is the regional characteristic. From one of the top *Cru
Classé* Provence estates.
VIN; HDR; HFW

*Mas de Gourgonnier Tradition Coteaux d'Aix-en-Provence,
Les Baux 1989*
2 £c NP ?

White wines from this region need to be made carefully to give
them fruit and character. Otherwise they can slide into dull
banality. This, made from Ugni Blanc, is only the third vintage of
white wines from the estate and has an intensely fruity nose and
precise clean flavour. Drink it young for maximum benefit.
HFW; OWC

Domaine St Cyriaque, Coteaux Varios, VDQS, 1989
2 £b NP V

Some Sauvignon in this to accompany the Ugni Blanc and
Semillon, but we could not really detect it in the taste. Nevertheless
a pleasant herby bouquet, good powerful flavour with more
resonance than often found in this region.
OWC; GJF

Rhône

Pierre André, Châteauneuf-du-Pape 1988/9
1 £d FESA VE
Silver Medal winner, Mâcon 1989. The Rhône is known

principally for its huge red wines, the whites being often overlooked — or when discovered, frequently rather mono-dimensional and lacking in life. However this is a delightful strong, firm and quite weighty wine — very classy. Bottling is carried out with a biodynamic approach, in relation to the phases of the moon. The quantity of wine produced per hectare is tiny, making this full of concentrated fruit flavour, rounded and lingering nicely in the mouth. The grapes used are Clairette, Bourlbenc, Grenache Blanc and Roussane, and final sulphur content is low at around 11 milligrams per litre. Excellent.

HDR; VIN; VRT

Domaine St Apollinaire, Côtes du Rhône Viognier 1987/88
3 £d/e DYN VE

We tasted the 1987, made solely from the Viognier grape, a speciality of the region, and found it rich in the mouth, with a lemony nose and excitingly bitter, nutty flavour. A delicious wine and like the white wine of Pierre André in Châteauneuf, made from vines producing a very small amount of top-quality fruit.

VRT; OWC

Château de Beaucastel, Châteauneuf-du-Pape 1987
1 £e IND V

From a blend of Rhône white wine grapes — predominantly Roussane with some Grenache Blanc, Bourlbenc and others — a light yellow colour and very aromatic bouquet, with excellent slightly fat flavour. Fine to drink now but will stand the test of time for a while yet.

HFW

Château de Beaucastel, Roussane, Vieille Vignes Châteauneuf-du-Pape 1986
2 £f IND V

Made solely from the Roussane grape and from vines that are 45 years old or more, this is frankly stunning. We tasted the 1988 vintage and found it to have exquisite integrated lemon, oak and citrus flavours in the bouquet and a long, cool flavour in the mouth. Very pale in colour; 'absolutely correct' was one comment.

HFW

Clos de l'Arbalastrier, St Joseph 1984
3 £d IND ?

Marsanne grapes, from a single hectare of vines, vinified in wooden barrels and then stored for 3 years before bottling. Very low sulphur, another of the top-quality wines from this region made organically. Forceful gold colour, big, generous flavour following the long fruity nose.

HFW

South West

Château le Barradis, Bergerac Sauvignon Sec
1 £b NP V

Grassy green colour and grassy green nose. Herbaceous fresh style, the Sauvignon grape character stands out nicely and has a crisp acidity to it, without being unbalanced. On special occasions at the estate they mix it in a special nose-shaped glass with a myrtle syrup called Myrano, after the character Cyrano de Bergerac.

HDR; VIN; WHI; BLA; CRS; BUP

Château le Barradis Monbazillac 1982/5/6/8
8 £c NP VE

A delicious richly sweet dessert wine, the 1982 vintage was described by the *Financial Times* as 'one of the best Monbazillacs on the market'. This estate produces very good dry white, as well as red and sparkling wines (not to mention grape juice and fruits), but the Monbazillac takes pride of place. The wines are superbly rich and honeyed, without being sickly sweet. Each vintage has a different shade of orangey yellow, becoming darker and more pronounced as the years pass. The 1982 is magnificent, the 1985 is a lighter colour, and the 1986 promises to be the best of the lot, being already darker than the 1982. The estate is on a hill overlooking the town of Bergerac, within a stone's throw of the great Château Monbazillac. The tasting room seems to be almost permanently open; if you are in the area do not forego the chance to sample their wares in the company of the flamboyant and idiosyncratic Jacques Victor Mornai, salesman and proselytizer extraordinaire.

1985: VRT; WHI; OWC; All vintages: HDR; VIN

Monbazillac, Domaine Monbouche 1988
8 £d UNIA ?

A slightly lighter style than the le Barradis, not quite the fullness

of body, but deliciously direct and clean. The difference lies in the equal quantities of Semillon and Sauvignon used here, the Sauvignon lightening the Semillon's weight and providing nice acidity as a counterbalance.
HFW

GERMANY

Baden

Grunerner Altenberg, Müller-Thurgau Kabinett, trocken, 1985
2 £c BIO ?

From a family that has been making wines since 1756, a bone-dry, direct tasting wine, deep green/yellow colour. Silver Medal winner at the Baden Wine Fair 1987.
OWC

Franken

Dettelbacher Berg Rondell, Müller-Thurgau QbA trocken, R & H Christ 1986
2 £d BIO ?

Franconia (Franken) is the most easterly wine-producing region in Germany, with the town of Würzburg in the middle. The wines have quite a distinctive earthy character, and are not all that frequently found in the UK. Popular in Germany because the style is quite different to other regions, it is drier and more akin to French dry whites. If you do see them they are instantly recognizable by their bottles, green flagons known as Bocksbeutel. This Müller-Thurgau from the ethereally-named R & H Christ is fairly typical of the grape, green-gold in colour with firm, medium weight.
OWC

Wipfelder Zehntgraf, Müller-Thurgau Kabinett, trocken, R & H Christ 1986
4 £d BIO ?

Dry wine with more specific aroma to the bouquet than the more basic QbA Müller-Thurgau from this estate, showing nice racy acidity and a decent length.
OWC

Wipfelder Zehntgraf, Kerner Kabinett trocken, R & H Christ 1986
2 £c BIO ?

The relative aristocracy of the Kerner grape gives a marked perfume nose with full body and spicy flavour.
OWC

Mosel

Maringer Sonnenuhr, Müller-Thurgau QbA trocken, Johannes Schneider 1987
2 £c BIO ?

From the most widely-planted of all grapes in Germany, in the dry style now making a comeback.
OWC

Elbling, QbA, Harald Steffens, Briedel, trocken, 1988
4 £c BIO V

A fresh light-bodied dry wine from the Elbling, one of Germany's oldest grape types. Lively acidity and delicate floral bouquet.
HFW; COW

Maringer Sonnenuhr, Riesling Kabinett trocken, Johannes Schneider 1987
2 £d BIO ?

A pale coloured wine with a strong character of the grape variety on the nose and the palate, in the dry style.
OWC

Nähe

Guldentaler Apostleberg, Müller-Thurgau Kabinett, trocken, Knodel 1988
2 £b BIO ?

Dry, light and fragrant. Easy and accessible.
OWC

Weisser Burgunder Kabinett trocken, Knodel 1986
4 £b BIO ?

The Pinot Blanc grape of France and Italy, here making a dry, grapey wine with full flavour.
OWC

Guldentaler Apostleberg, Müller-Thurgau QbA, trocken, Knodel 1987
2 £b BIO ?
An easy quaffing wine with a dry, fruity style.
OWC

Windesheimer Rosenberg, Riesling QbA trocken, Knodel 1987
2 £b BIO ?
Reasonably priced, a wine with a strong bouquet of the grape and plenty of flavour, with some acidity in the mouth.
OWC

Windesheimer Rosenberg, Riesling Kabinett trocken, Knodel 1988
2 £c BIO ?
A grade up the quality levels from the QbA wine, more sugar in the 'grape must' giving it an overall fuller flavour and weight. Greenish colour and strident flavour.
OWC

Windesheimer Schlosskapelle, Riesling Kabinett trocken, Knodel 1988
2 £c BIO ?
After Müller-Thurgau, Riesling and Silvaner are the principal grapes of the Nähe region to the north of the Rhine river. Here in its currently fashionable dry style.
OWC

Guldentaler Honigberg, Silvaner QbA trocken, Knodel 1986
2 £c BIO ?
In litre bottles, a light medium-bodied wine, with restrained bouquet.
OWC

Windesheimer Rosenberg, Kerner Spätlese halbtrocken, Knodel 1985
3 £c BIO ?
'Half-dry', a richly intense wine with plenty of the character of the grape.
OWC

Windesheimer Rosenberg, Scheurebe Kabinett halbtrocken, Knodel 1988
2 £c BIO ?

Quite overt bouquet and rounded flavour, again showing that this grape variety can produce fine wines.
OWC

Windesheimer Rosenberg, Kerner QbA, Knodel 1987
4 £b BIO ?

Showing the style of this grape variety well, a light to medium bodied wine with lively fruit bouquet.
OWC

Guldentaler St Martin, Riesling Kabinett, Knodel 1986
4 £b BIO ?

Soft, greeny-gold colour wine, not too sweet with pleasantly fragrant grapes.
OWC

Windesheimer Rosenberg, Gewürztraminer Kabinett, Knodel 1987
4 £c BIO ?

An elegant wine from the spicy Gewürztraminer, extravagantly floral and nicely grapey.
OWC

Windesheimer Rosenberg, Riesling/Gewürztraminer Auslese, Knodel 1985
7 £d BIO ?

A blend of these two classic grapes makes a richly sweet wine with an intriguing character. Many different fruit flavours interlace; a somewhat subdued bouquet but promising more as it evolves.
OWC

Rheinhessen

Bereich Nierstein QbA trocken, Konrad Knodel 1988
2 £c BIO VE

Sold in litre bottles, one of the few organic wines from the famous name of Nierstein. A ripe fruity aroma and soft fruity acidity. Easy to drink on its own and with food.
OWC

Kerner QbA trocken, Sander 1987
1 £b BOW VE

From the village of Mittenheim between Worms and Mainz, the Sander family have been making wine for generations. Their 10 hectares produce nicely integrated wines, full flavoured and fruity. Over the years they have received many awards for the high quality of their products. Organic methods were begun in the 1950s, before later moving over to full organic status under the BOW. This wine is lightly spiced with a nice aroma and some elegance. Dry.
SED

Flonheimer Klostergarten, Kerner Spätlese trocken, H Thiel 1986
1 £d BOW VE

Dry, with reasonable acidity coming through to balance the fruit.
ROD

Biebelnheimer Pilgerstein, Reichensteiner Spätlese trocken, Knodel 1986
6 £c BIO ?

A dry wine with good body, a long finish and a delicate overall flavour. Not a very highly rated grape variety in the pecking order of the great and the good, it is the result of a family tree, involving vine varieties from several different countries. This 'Euro' variety pops up quite often in English vineyards, and is usually solid rather than exotic.
OWC

Riesling QbA trocken, Schonhals 1987
2 £b BOW VE

Classic Riesling style, clean as a whistle — crisp, fresh and fruity.
SED

Silvaner QbA trocken, D. Werner 1988
2 £b ANOG VE

Dry, lightly balanced wine, pale yellow in colour. Uncomplicated straightforward stuff.
OWC

Uffhofener La Roche Riesling, Kabinett trocken, H Thiel 1984
1 £d BOW VE

Now nicely mature, a strongly flavoured example of the grape type, probably at its best. In litre bottles.
ROD

Uffhofener Pfaffenberg, Silvaner Kabinett trocken, H Thiel 1988
1 £c BOW VE

Dry Silvaner with strong aroma and good length of finish. Available in both 70cl and litre bottles.

ROD

Weissburgunder Kabinett trocken, Sander 1988
2 £c BOW VE

The Weissburgunder of Germany is the same as the Pinot Blanc of Alsace in France and, most notably, Pinot Bianco in Italy. This is a solid dry wine, lightly aromatic, easy and undemanding. 'Long lingering palate of fresh fruit salad' according to the distributor. But what does he have in his fruit salads? Mangos? Gooseberries? Grapes?

SED

Gimmeldinger Meerspinne QbA trocken, 1986. Litre bottles
2 £c BIO ?

We have not tasted this wine and the distributor's note is the briefest and most succinct of all tasting notes: 'Great for parties!'

OWC

Flonheimer Klostergarten Kerner, Spätlese halbtrocken, H Thiel 1985
3 £c BOW VE

Nice deep golden hue, medium dry, floral bouquet.

ROD

Riesling, QbA, Dienheimer Paterhof, Ludwigshöhe, halbtrocken, Dr Becker 1986
3 £c ROAWR ?

A full and tangy bouquet heralds a rich fruit character. Nicely balanced.

HFW; COW

Dienheimer Paterhof Riesling Kabinett, Bruder Dr Becker 1989, halbtrocken
3 £c BOW V

Dr Becker is one of the best organic growers in Germany. Classic Riesling character here made in a medium-dry style.

ODD

St Ursula Rivaner QmP 1989 halbtrocken
3 £b BOW ?
This wine was about to be introduced as we went to press, and is untasted by us. Other wines from the St Ursula Weinkellerei have been very good. Rivaner is a synonym for Müller-Thurgau, not always the noblest of grape varieties, so it will be interesting to see what they have produced.
SAN; BUP

Silvaner QbA, halbtrocken, D. Werner 1988
2 £b ANOG VE
As for the *trocken* wine, but with more natural grape sugars present making a medium-dry wine.
OWC

Müller-Thurgau QbA, D. Werner 1989
3 £b ANOG VE
A firm almondy flavour from Germany's most widely-planted grape variety, with a nice nose, a good greenish colour and, as seems to be generally the character from this estate, a well-balanced and harmonious wine.
VIN; HDR

Sylvaner, QbA, Ludwigshöhe Teufelskopf, Dr Becker 1986
5 £c ROAWR ?
Another excellent wine from the laudable Dr Becker, and this Riesling has a spicy bouquet and strong upfront flavour.
HFW; COW; WRK

St Ursula Scheurebe, 1989
5 £b BOW VE
Made from the wines of five different organic growers and assembled by the St Ursula Weinkellerei, the wine is medium-dry with a distinctive grape character. Described in *Which? Wine Monthly* as having 'toffee'd fruit on the nose, a slight spritz, and a honeyed palate which is balanced by a well-judged acidity'.
SAF; BUP

Scheurebe Kabinett, QbA, Ludwigshöhe Dr Becker 1987
6 £c ROAWR ?
'Delightful nose of lemons and spices, quite unusual style, racy and rich.' So say the importers. An intriguing and catchy wine from this small and high quality estate.
HFW; COW

Flonheimer Klostergarten, Bacchus Kabinett, D. Werner, 1989
4 £b ANOG VE

Wildly rough bouquet and enticingly balanced fruit and acidity on
the palate. Lovely ripe grape character; a 'medium' wine of real life
and interest. 8.5 per cent alcohol. Bacchus is now a well-established
variety in Germany — aptly named after the god — and is the result
of crossing Müller-Thurgau with an already hybrid Silvaner-
Riesling vine. The best of all worlds! Renowned as being low in
acidity, this example is quite the opposite, with fine acid balance.
HDR; VIN

**Bechtolsheimer Klosterberg, Faberrebe Kabinett, Konrad Knodel
1987**
4 £c BIO ?

The Faber (or Faberrebe as it is called here) has the exciting
characteristics of Riesling, showing life and fruit in abundance. It
is a hybrid crossing from Weissburgunder and Müller-Thurgau
parentage. This one, made in the soft and grapey medium to
medium sweet style, carries both fruit and body.
OWC

Böchinger Rosenkrantz, Kerner Kabinett, Knodel 1987
4 £c BIO ?

Litre bottles for regular consumption! Pale yellow colour but good
bouquet and soft finish, the Kerner grape provides a classy base to
the wine.
OWC

Dienheimer Tafelstein Kabinett, Bruder Dr Becker
4 £b BOW ?

Safeway have collected together four different wines from Dr
Becker, all of Kabinett level quality, and they list them under the
single title. An ingenious way for a large company to cope with the
limited and varied production of organic growers, the wines
comprise Scheurebe, Riesling, Schönburger halbtrocken and
Kerner halbtrocken. Styles therefore vary between grape variety and
also between sweet and medium-dry. The vegetarian/vegan issue is
complex here — the Riesling and Scheurebe are suitable for vegans;
the Kerner and Schönburger are fined using bentonite, kieselguhr
and gelatine. Gelatine can be made from bones but is increasingly
made from vegetable sources. But we do not know which in

which in this particular case! Becker maintains a consistently high standard of winemaking.

SAF

Flonheimer Geisterberg, Scheurebe Kabinett, H Thiel 1986
4 £c BOW VE

An everyday wine, available in both 70cl and 100cl, from the Scheurebe grape. Scheurebe is another of the 'new' breed of grapes produced in Germany from crossing two other varieties, in this case Silvaner and Riesling. Not a bad parenthood for this climate, and the grape is capable of making some very fine wines. This example has fullish flavour and marked bouquet.

ROD

Scheurebe Kabinett, Schonhals 1987
8 £b BOW V

Light, fresh and smooth, rounded and with a delightful sweet finish.

SED

Erbes Budesheimer Vogelsang, Gewürztraminer Spätlese, H Thiel 1982
6 £d BOW VE

Very delicious Gewürztraminer, strong spicy flavour. Matured in oak for three years, a powerful, heady wine with a rich, long finish.

ROD

Flonheimer Adelberg, Kerner Spätlese, Gebruder Werner 1988
6 £c ANOG VE

A fairly sweet wine, full of succulent rich grape flavours. Described by *Which? Wine Monthly* as having an 'elegant palate, not as racy as Riesling but clean and honeyed with fine acid balance'.

SAF

Gau-Odernheimer Petersberg, Kerner Spätlese 1988
6 £c BIO ?

From a grape variety that is something of a modern-day success story. The Kerner is a crossing between Riesling and the red grape type, Trollinger, and is said to be the most similar to Riesling. It can produce very high-quality wines with quite a racy character. This is light in colour with medium weight and a spicy bouquet.

OWC

Ensheimer Kachelberg, Riesling/Weissburgunder Spätlese, H Thiel 1983
6 £c BOW VE

Having had time to mature and knit together, the flavour is nicely integrated. Good floral aroma, nicely balanced, with sufficient acidity to counter the natural grape flavours.
ROD

Lonsheimer Mandelburg, Wurzer Spätlese, D. Werner 1989
6 £b ANOG VE

Very pronounced floral bouquet, appealing sweet fruit and retaining a lightness that enhances the overall flavour. The grape variety is not widely planted and is mostly found in this region. Being a cross between Gewürztraminer and Müller-Thurgau, it carries a fullness and spice that work well. Nicely concentrated without being over sweet.
HDR; VIN

Erbes Budesheimer Vogelsang Gewürztraminer, Auslese, H Thiel 1976
7 £e BOW VE

Nice to see the availability of a genuinely aged organic Auslese. The natural weight of the wine has rounded well and produced a delightfully mellow flavour with great depth of character. Powerful and long-lasting flavours.
ROD

Flonheimer Geisterberg Morio-Muskat, Auslese, H Thiel 1976
7 £e BOW VE

Morio-Muskat is a crossing of Silvaner and Pinot Blanc, carried out by one Peter Morio. Aptly named, the variety can produce wines with a bouquet to rival the Muscat, being very highly perfumed. This well-matured Auslese has a powerful rich, grapey nose that carries through to the flavour. National Gold Medal winner.
ROD

Flonheimer Geisterberg, Optima Auslese, D. Werner 1989
7 £b ANOG VE

A richly honeyed wine, from late-picked grapes. An example of weight and character without cloying sweetness. The comments on this were all to do with its rounded, balanced character. Delicate, lightly floral bouquet.
HDR; VIN

Uffhofener Pfaffenberg Huxelrebe/Malvasier Beerenauslese, H Thiel 1976
➤ 8 £f BOW VE

National Gold Medal winner. A rare and very rich dessert wine from overripe, noble rot-affected, top-quality grapes. The wine is a blend of two grapes, Huxelrebe and Malvasia, the former a crossing named after the German grower who first developed its use, Fritz Huxel. Huxelrebe can produce high sugar content in the juice prior to fermentation, allowing the possibility of big, rich wines such as this.

ROD

Dreikonigs-Strohwein, Riesling trockenbeerenauslese, H Thiel 1970
➤ 9 £f BOW VE

At the time of going to press this wine was being sold by importer and ex-miner David Rodgers in Barnsley for a mere £158.27 per bottle, and these only 70cl. Nevertheless, if you are going to try one of the mightiest wine types that the world can offer, it's nice to see that the grape variety is the best available. Riesling is the premier grape of Germany, befitting a premier wine. This is, we are told, hugely rich and concentrated, as one would expect from these specially late picked selected grapes. In deference to David's profitability we did not ask for a sample.

ROD

Ensheimer Kachelberg Spätburgunder trockenbeerenauslese-Eiswein, H Thiel 1981
➤ 9 £f BOW VE

Gold Medal Winner. This is about as richly sweet as you can get. The trockenbeerenauslese quality of grape — those that have been left to shrivel to a raisin-like state and massive sugar concentration, usually after attack by noble rot — picked at the frozen Eiswein stage in the winter morning takes us into the land of dreams. Stunningly luscious, concentrated and honeyed, a half bottle of this marvellous wine is going to set you back nearly £50.

ROD

Flonheimer Geisterberg, Scheurebe Beerenauslese-Eiswein, H Thiel 1981
➤ 8 £f BOW VE

Aromatic and catchy, reasonable acidity enhanced by the Eiswein collection of the grapes, already very richly concentrated in

Berenauslese quality. The price is for 37.5cl bottles, making this
very expensive, and quite delicious.
ROD

*Uffhofener Pfaffenberg, Silvaner Beerenauslese-Eiswein, H Thiel
1976*
8 £f BOW VE
Regional Gold Medal winner. Another deeply rich wine with
interlaced complexity of weighty flavours. The Silvaner character
produces only a light floral nose but the depth of the flavour is
excellent.
ROD

Rheinpfalz

Pfälzer Landwein, Weingut Fritz Breiling
2 £b BIO VE
A dryish wine for everyday — 'Landwein' is the German equivalent
of 'Vin de Pays'. Some acidity and a lightly floral bouquet make it
open, mellow and friendly. Made from Müller-Thurgau and
Sylvaner grapes.
VRT; SED

Mussbacher Eselshaut, Silvaner QbA 1986, Knodel
2 £c BIO ?
Good length and medium weight with full fruit.
OWC

Mussbacher Glockenzehnt, Kerner Kabinett halbtrocken, 1986
3 £b BIO ?
Medium-dry wine, balanced and bright.
OWC

Maikammer Mandelhohe, Scheurebe Kabinett, F. Breiling, 1989
4 £c BIO VE
An outstanding vintage, this wine is made from late-picked grapes
affected by noble rot and is a rich deep golden colour. Fine musty
bouquet, honeyed, oily, complex flavour. Nice.
SED

Müller-Thurgau Spätlese, F. Breiling 1983
7 £c BIO VE
Aged in large oak barrels prior to bottling, though more for natural

ageing than to impart any flavour. A grapey medium-sweet wine with a heady scent of apples and pears, well-balanced with fine fruity acidity. A particularly good vintage.

SED

ITALY

Arneis di Monta', Renato Rabezzana 1988
2 £d SS VE

Renato Rabezzana is a slightly folklorish and eccentric figure in the Italian wine world, a proud traditionalist. A man who has stuck with little-known and not commercially sought-after local grape varieties, retaining a strong individualistic principle. Here he uses the unfamiliar Arneis grape to make a marvellously intense, smooth, almost appley wine. Light golden in colour and with a slight spritz.

ORG

Bianco del Piemonte Serra Massone, P.Gozzelino 1988/9
3 £b AIAB VE

The grower of these grapes has no cellar or vinification equipment of his own. So he grows his organic grapes and then whisks them off to someone else's cellar to make the wine. This one is a white made exclusively from three red grape varieties, and has a quite unusual and distinctive style. Dry to medium-dry, with a slight spritz, full-bodied and fruity.

ORG

Bianco di Pontelungo, Villa Angiolina 1988/9
2 £b SS VE

From the small Chianti Putto estate of Villa Angiolina, where mother and daughter look after the wine side of things and the father and son work elsewhere. Although predominantly a red wine producer, the whites show promise. This one is from Trebbiano and Malvasia grapes, and made with quantities of sulphur dioxide way below the amount approved even by the organic association they belong to. Nice green to lemon colour, with a creamy, citrusy bouquet which is also how the wine tastes. Pleasant weight of flavour, good finish and sufficient fruit to make this a wine we enjoyed very much.

ORG; VRT

Bianco San Pietro, Guerrieri-Rizzardi 1988/89
5 £b IND V

From the well-established and increasingly popular estate created
by Count Carlo Rizzardi. They produce a wide range of wines from
different vineyard sites, this being blended from both traditional
and modern grape varieties — Tokay, Garganega, Semillon and
Chardonnay. The wine is dry, with a definite crispness, backed up
by soft fruit flavours.
VRT; HFW

Bianco, F. Croissant 1989
1 £b BIO VE

Herbaceous, fresh dry wine, only 10 per cent alcohol, to drink
young. From the Trebbiano grape.
SED

**Chardonnay di Val Lagarina, Vino de Tavola, Guerrieri-
Rizzardi 1987/8/9**
4 £b IND V

Made from the Chardonnay grape, the wine has a bright, light
yellow colour. Good Chardonnay character, dry, lemony and light.
There is some difference between the vintages, but the general style
is consistent. Best young, the wine has not been aged in oak, thus
leaving the grape flavours to vouch for themselves and adding to the
light fruity character. Do not be misled by the Vino da Tavola status
— this is one of those situations where Italian quality designation
is not a true reflection of the quality of the wine.
HFW; COW; VRT

Moscato d'Asti DOC, P. Gozzelino 1988
7 £b AIAB VE

Medium sweet 'frizzante' (semi-sparkling) wine from the
wonderful and intensely grapey Moscato. A nice spicy aroma. Only
5 per cent alcohol and delicious.
ORG

Narciso de' Poeti, Villa Angiolina
1 £c SS VE

A rich, creamy flavour predominates in this oak-aged wine, buttery
and round. Dark gold colour, strong wood smell in the bouquet.
Individually numbered bottles, the daffodil on the label is the
Narcissus of the Poets in the name.
ORG; VRT

Pinot Bianco, Zanette
2 £b AIAB/BIODYN VE

From producers with biodynamic grapes but a reluctance to turn them into wine! This is a simple, uncomplicated wine, semi-sparkling and easy to drink.
ORG

Poggio alle Rocche, il Palagio 1988/9
1 £b AIAB VE

Light, cool, fresh dry white from Tuscany. The second-string wine from this producer, often harvested early to retain the freshness and delicacy of the wine. From Trebbiano and Vernaccia grapes.
ORG

Prosecco del Veneto, Zanette
2 £b AIAB/BIODYN VE

Also semi-sparkling, and similar to his Pinot Bianco but with a slightly nuttier flavour.
ORG

Soave Classico, Guerrieri-Rizzardi 1988/89
5 £b IND V

A high-quality example of this very popular wine, made from Gargenega and Trebbiano grapes. Delicate, light and fragrant, with an enticing fruit bouquet and pale yellow colour.
VRT; HFW; COW

Soave Costeggiola DOC Classico, Guerrieri-Rizzardi 1988/89
2 £c IND VE

This is their single-vineyard Soave, from Costeggiola, made from vines with lower yields. Good fullness of fruit, smooth and with a firm fragrant bouquet.
VRT

Tenuto San Vito, Bianco Toscano, Roberto Drighi 1988/9
1 £b SS VE

A very open and accessible wine, light straw colour with hints of gold. Vivid, dry and very alive with fruity flavours. From Trebbiano and Malvasia grapes.
HDR; VIN

Tenuto San Vito, Verdiglio, Roberto Drighi 1988/9
1 £b SS VE

Made from Verdicchio grapes, this is a much darker green colour and has an altogether stronger, more pronounced flavour than their other white, the Bianco Toscano. A powerful nutty bouquet and rich full flavour with a creamy, almondy background.
HDR; VIN

Trebbiano di Poggio Antico 1988/89
2 £b AIAB/D VE

Poggio Antico is a co-operatively run organic farm, having crops and livestock as well as wine. Inspired by fundamentalist Catholic beliefs, the commmunity seek to live out their ideals in a practical way. This white is fruity and nutty, at the medium end of dry. The communards are not keen on alcohol, because of its negative role in social relations, and would prefer to sell all their organic grapes as juice, or simply as grapes. But the demand for wine is higher.
ORG

Vernaccia di San Gimignano DOC, il Palagio 1988/9
1 £b AIAB VE

Vernaccia is the grape type. From Tuscany, to be drunk young and fresh. Dry, golden, and in herby style. The producer was a nuclear physicist before being an organic grower!
ORG

Vinsanto il Cavaliere, Villa Angiolina
4 £e SS VE

Medium-dry, oak-aged and very exotic. This is a Tuscan speciality, made from late-harvested and specially dried grapes. The result is high alcohol — 15 per cent here — and an intriguing combination of background sugar and dry, sherry-like taste. This example is quite sweet compared to the San Vito, more towards port and after dinner drinking. Heavy, dark colour. Delicious, of course.
ORG

Vin Santo, Tenuta San Vito 1985
3 £e SS VE

The Vin Santo from this estate is slightly drier than that down the road at Villa Angiolina, more towards sherry than port, but really unique to itself. 15 per cent alcohol, either an aperitif or dessert wine, full-bodied and intriguing. We drank it 'in situ' with locally

produced rough bread which had been rubbed with fresh garlic —
recommended.
  HDR; VIN

AUSTRALIA

Crouchen, Botobolar Vineyard 1988
2 £c NASAA VE

The Crouchen grape (also known as the Claire Riesling) is not well-
known in the UK. The wine has become smoother with some time
to age in the bottle, and has a hint of tropical fruits in the flavour.
Slightly waxy, rather like some Semillon-based wines from
Bordeaux, it is robust for a white. While it has good structure it
perhaps lacks freshness and zest.
  VRT; HDR; VIN; SED

Riesling Traminer, Botobolar Vineyard 1989
2 £b NASAA VE

From a blend of Riesling and Traminer grapes, the best white wine
from this vineyard. Good fruity bouquet, crisp fresh flavour which
is richly full bodied.
  VRT

ENGLAND

Avalon Seyval 1989
1 £b SA VE

Dr Hugh Tripp has seven acres in the Vale of Avalon, equally
divided between vines and apple trees. The vines are predominantly
Seyval and Schoenberger, the Seyval being particularly suitable to
organic vine growing in England because it is resistant to mildew.
His wine bar and farm shop are open each afternoon to visitors and
you can pick your own organic soft fruits.

  This is possibly the driest wine in the listing. A lot of
conventionally produced English wines can be a bit dull and
blandly medium in style. Not this. It is reminiscent of good Gros
Plant, or possibly Muscadet, in France's Loire valley. Very high but
just contained acidity, balanced by lovely fresh fruit. The Seyval
grape grows well in the English climate, being more resistant than
most to the problems of mould. The wine contains approximately

20mg/litre of SO_2, and is filtered once before bottling. It should mellow and become more rounded and integrated in flavour as it ages.

HDR; VIN

Sedlescombe Müller-Thurgau 1989
4 £c/d SA VE

Sedlescombe vineyard was founded in 1979 by husband and wife team Roy and Irma Cook. Now with 10 acres, it is the largest verified organic vineyard in the UK, has a shop stocking organic wines from many different countries, and acts as host for eager participants on the Working Weekends on Organic Farms association. This wine is medium-dry, with a light scented character and generous flavour. 10.5 per cent alcohol.

OWC; SED; VRT

Sedlescombe Gutenborner 1989
1 £c SA VE

The 1986 vintage of this wine was heralded by Jancis Robinson MW, a leading wine journalist, as tasting 'like a rather seductive Tokay d'Alsace: smokey, relatively full-bodied and pungent but with sufficient acidity'. The 1986 was medium, whereas the 1989 and 1990 vintages are crisp and dry, but retaining the essential character.

SED

Sedlescombe Ortega 1989
2 £c SA VE

One of the more unusual grapes to be grown here, the Ortega is of German origin. This example is dry, soft, and with a slight elderflower bouquet. 11.5 per cent alcohol.

SED; OWC

Sedlescombe Huxel 1989
2 £d SA VE

A 'green apples' type of wine, good tangy acidity but with enough fruit to balance things out. High in alcohol for an English wine at 12.5 per cent. Probably the driest and steeliest of Roy Cook's whites.

SED

Sedlescombe Gewürztraminer 1989
◼▸ 2 £d SA VE

The collector's item of the Sedlescombe range. From late-picked grapes with a high sugar content, but dry as the sugar is fermented out. Fragrant bouquet smelling lightly of fresh roses, the wine is full-bodied, rich, almost peachy in flavour. A delightful wine to drink on its own.

SED

Sedlescombe Reichensteiner 1989
2 £c/d SA VE

The Reichensteiner may not be the most elegant-sounding grape in the world, but this is a real 1992 offering. Grown in Sussex, the grape is a crossing from the German Müller-Thurgau, French Madeleine Angevine and Italian Calabrese! The wine is much more interesting than many from this variety — and many English wines in general — with an off-dry character and mild fruit.

VRT; SED

HUNGARY

Leanyka — Szekszardi MG Kombinat 1989
2 £a/b EKO VE

The Leanyka (or little girl) is the name of the grape. This wine is well made and creamy in flavour, slightly buttery and with a honeyed bouquet. Excellent value for everyday drinking.

VRT; HDR; VIN

NEW ZEALAND

Riesling, Millton Vineyard 1988/89
3 £c/d BIOGROW V

The Millton vineyard was created by James and Annie Millton in 1984 in Gisborne, on the east coast of North Island. They use organic and biodynamic methods in order to produce the best fruit from which to make high quality wines. To date the quality of all the vintages tasted is exceptional across the range of wines. This Riesling is a weighty, powerfully scented wine. With a dark green colour and a bouquet of wild flowers the body of the wine lasts well in the mouth. Very well balanced and towards medium dry.

VRT; HDR; VIN; OWC; SED

Chenin Blanc, Millton Vineyard 1989
2 £c/d BIOGROW V

The Chenin Blanc grape suffers most from the climate here, being susceptible to attack by mould. The 1990 vintage was devastated in this way, so the quantity available is very restricted. But the quality is not impaired. Just as with the Chardonnay from this estate, a magnificient and engaging wine, bursting with fruit flavour and showing just what an enormous variety of styles the Chenin Blanc grape can produce. The 1989 is, as with their Chardonnay, an elegant style. Excellent length of finish, drier than their '88, with greater acidity, the 1989 is more concentrated and centred in character, and an extra degree higher in alcohol at 12.5 per cent. Top class wine. Silver Medal International Wine Challenge 1990 (1988 vintage).

VRT; HDR; VIN; OWC; SED

Chardonnay, Millton Vineyard 1988/9
3 £d BIOGROW V

The 1988 came top of an organic wine tasting carried out by the *Independent on Sunday* in August 1990. It is a hugely generous, rounded, pineappley wine. Very upfront strong flavour, juicy, with great weight. A really packed mouthful. The 1989 has been made in a slightly different style and does not have the same immediate flavour, but is creamier, more delicate and elegant — a more sophisticated wine altogether. Higher in alcohol and lower in residual sugar than the 1988, and with a longer, lingering finish that really seals the quality. A fascinating example of the difference that can emerge between vintages, and both excellent in their own ways.

VRT; HDR; VIN; OWC; EDB

PORTUGAL

Vinho Verde de Lafoes, Quinta de Commenda, 1989
1 £c AGROBIO ?

If you have never tasted real Vinho Verde in Portugal, prepare yourself for a change of expectations. Most of the exported stuff is sweetened for the Euro-palate, but the real wine is tartly dry, crisp and fresh, like Gros Plant from the Loire. This is, to our knowledge, the only verified organic wine made in Portugal. Do not be put off by the price — high quality genuine single estate (Quinta) wines are not cheap. This is best drunk as fresh as possible, when it has a

creamy, dry style and light colour.
VRT

SPAIN

Penedes, DO Blanco Novell, Albet i Noya 1987/8
1 £b VS VE

The 1988 won a Silver Medal in the regional Penedes tasting competition and is excellent, and markedly better than the 1987. A dry, balanced wine with a slightly nutty background flavour and distinct taste of the Macabeu and Chardonnay grapes. From the same producer as the Cava.
HDR; VIN

Sierra Morena, Vino Palido 15.5 per cent
1 £c UMBELLA V

Not, as you might think, a fortified wine. This tastes just like dry, Fino, sherry. But it is not called sherry because it is produced in Cordoba, just outside the Jerez region. But you would be unlikely to tell the difference from the taste. Very crisp, dry and light, with a fine amber colour. High in alcohol, this unfortunately means higher tax and so raises the price. The producers say they cannot reduce the alcohol content without affecting the quality of the wine.
HDR; VIN; OWC

RED WINES

FRANCE

Alsace

Pinot Noir, Eugène Meyer, 1986
A £c D VE

It's not all that common to find red Alsace wines in the UK, but anything from this exceptional winemaker is worth looking at closely. Made without the addition of sulphur, from 100 per cent Pinot Noir, it is light and distinctive.
  HFW; COW; WHI

Bordeaux

Château la Chapelle Maillard, Bordeaux 1988/9
C £b NP VE

Jean-Luc and Renée Devert have a very tidy little 8-hectare estate in Bordeaux producing a good white as well as this spicy red. Bags of natural fruit flavours interlacing each other, the wine has an engaging character. Well structured, the integration of the grape varieties — 40 per cent Merlot, 40 per cent Cabernet Franc and 20 per cent Cabernet Sauvignon — produces a good rich wine which is fine now and will continue to improve for a few years yet. The 1989 vintage won a Silver Medal at the Paris Concours Generale.
  VIN; HDR

Château la Croix Simon, Bordeaux 1988
C £b NP VE

Good middle of the table stuff, very pleasant and with decent fruit. A nicely made wine, very typical of the region.
  OWC

Château des Hautes Combes, Bordeaux 1989
C £b FESA No
Ramon Garcia produces a wine for drinking young; he is one of many in Bordeaux for whom the possibility of ageing clarets is increasingly difficult as demand outstrips supply. His wine is lightly jammy, fresh and fruity, a juicy wine of medium body. From the Merlot, Cabernet Sauvignon and Cabernet Franc grapes.
VRT; OWC

Château Large-Malartic, Bordeaux 1988
C £b IND VE
A warm, full-bodied fruity claret from Merlot, Cabernet Sauvignon and Cabernet Franc grapes, made for early, easy drinking.
WWW

Château la Maubastit, Bordeaux 1988
C £b FESA ?
M Bernous is high ranking in the FESA organization and seems to be a key force in the promotion of the 'Claire Vallée' marketing company which seeks to distribute the products of FESA members. His wine is quite unusual in style, with rich cinnamon flavours and plenty of spice.
OWC

Château du Moulin de Peyronin, Bordeaux 1988
C £b UNIA V
Plummy fruit is the first impression from this wine. Medium-bodied, made to mature quite early so it is already open and accessible. A good everyday claret, predominantly Merlot.
HDR; VIN

Château Moulin de Romage, St Foy Bordeaux 1989
C £b NP VE
Youthful 50 per cent each of Cabernet Sauvignon and Merlot grapes, straightforward easy drinking claret, which could do with a little time to develop.
HFW; VRT

Organic Claret, Château Vieux-Georget, Bordeaux 1988
C £b UNIA V
Predominantly Cabernet Sauvignon with Cabernet Franc and a

little Merlot, which is a change from the usual blend in this part of Bordeaux, where the Merlot predominates. The 1986 vintage, selected as a *Which? Wine Monthly* Red of the Month, was described as 'a generous claret, deep ruby in colour . . . ripe and easy . . .' The 1988 continues this open style, with plenty of fruit and flavour, nicely rounded, with strong background structure. Well made.

ASD

Château Renaissance, Bordeaux 1989
☞ C £b NP VE

Gérard Descrambes is a good friend of Ramon Garcia at Château des Hautes Combes, and their wines are not dissimilar in style. Gerard's has more body, being weightier and with plenty of coarse ripe fruit. Nice jammy bouquet, loads of character but rarely a chance for the wine to age as it is all snatched up and quaffed early on. From Merlot and Cabernet grapes in the St Emilion region.

VIN; HDR

Clos Grand Plantier, Bordeaux 1987/88
☞ C £b FESA V

Well-balanced easy claret, with a fruity blackcurrant bouquet. Nice peppery flavour with caramel background.

VRT

Domaine du Bourdieu, Bordeaux 1987
C £c FNAB VE

Slightly unusual for this type of wine in that it has an equal proportion of Merlot and Cabernet Sauvignon, with some Cabernet Franc. Aged in oak for 4 months. Nice structure and harmonious style, better than average length. Patrick Boudon produces wines with a number of different labels, 'Bourdieu' being his principal wine.

WHI

Domaine Sainte Anne, Bordeaux 1988
C £b FNAB VE

Another label from Patrick Boudon near Targon. For this wine the blend is from vines grown on a different site. 40 per cent Cabernet Sauvignon and 60 per cent evenly distributed between Merlot and Cabernet Franc. A supple, fruity, light and easy wine.

WHI

Les Vieilles Garennes, Bordeaux 1989
C £b FNAB VE

M Boudon is a man with many different colours, and this is another wine from the stable that brings us Domaine de Bourdieu, Domaine Sainte Anne and Château Haut-Mallet. No doubting his skill as a quality winemaker, this is a decent upfront everyday wine.
WHI

Château Bossuet, Bordeaux Supérieur 1985
C £c IND ?

Predominantly Merlot with the usual Cabernet balance, a strong blackcurrant and oak bouquet. The wine has a smooth, silky texture. Good value.
HFW

Château Coursou, Bordeaux Supérieur 1987/9
C £b FESA V

Merlot and the Cabernets again; this is a good little estate. The 1987 is a nice, easy drinking claret; the 1989 is at present a bit rough at the edges but with loads of peppery, spicy fruit and nice structure. The predominance of the Merlot will aid early maturation. A popular style of wine and high quality.
HFW; COW; VRT

Château Haut-Mallet, Bordeaux Supérieur 1987
C £c FNAB V

The Château Haut-Mallet label is the pick of Patrick Boudon's range, being the product of small parcels of land in the best position and from the oldest plots. Cabernet Sauvignon is predominant and the wines are oak-aged for 9–12 months. This vintage has a ruby colour and plenty of intense fruit flavour and is drinking nicely now.
HFW; WHI

Château la Blanquerie Bordeaux Supérieur, 1986
C £b IND V

1986 was the last vintage before M Rougier signed his contract with Nature et Progrès. He had already been using organic methods independently for 20 years. This is a very fine claret, rounded, smooth and deliciously warm. Almost a textbook example of how to make this kind of wine.
VIN; HDR

Château Le Maubastit, Bordeaux Supérieur, 1988
➧ D £b FESA VE

A very untypical flavour for red Bordeaux, but highly intriguing.
Lots of interesting different flavours combine — mixed spice and
wild berries to name but two. Quite a big, rounded wine, with
further development in the bottle possible. Unusual and good with
strong foods.
SAF

Château Moulin Saint Magne, Bordeaux Supérieur, Côtes de Castillon 1987
C £b NP ?

This was not a highly-regarded vintage in Bordeaux, but this wine
is very drinkable, with good fruit and structure. Côtes de Castillon
is a small Appellation area around the town of Castillon-la-Bataille
within the larger Bordeaux region.
OWC

Château de Prade, Bordeaux Supérieur, 1986/8
➧ C £b BIOPLAMPAC VE

Isnel Fournier, proprietor of Château de Prade, is something of a
legend in the organic wine world of Bordeaux, a doughty fighter
against bureaucracy and very much his own man. A passionate
believer in the organic method, he has in the past left organic
organizations because he feels they are not strict enough. Like Guy
Bossard in the Loire, earlier vintages of his wine (especially the
1983) were instrumental with UK consumers in establishing the
reputation of organic wines as also being of good quality. His 1983
was scintillating; the two vintages now available mirror the region's
general style for these years. The 1986 is, we feel, ultimately going
to last longer and become the better of the two, but at present it
is a bit closed up and steely. Time will serve it well. The 1988 on
the other hand is better for drinking now, a delightfully mellow,
soft and balanced wine. Both vintages can be smooth and are full
of fruit. Reliably excellent.
VRT; ORG; SED; VIN; HDR; EDB; WAI(88)

Château du Puy Bordeaux Supérieur (many vintages 1976-1987)
➧ C £c UNIA/NP No

Unique in the organic world, this ancient Château has a long list
of old vintages available for commercial sale. The wines are drunk
in the French Assembly (without any noticeable improvement in

the representatives' decision-making prowess, according to another producer!) and the bottles for each vintage come individually wrapped in different coloured tissue paper. They are sealed with wax in place of the usual lead capsule, and the overall presentation is of a highly crafted and superieur product. M Amoreau has been cultivating his vines organically since 1945 and tells us he is one of the earliest organic growers, if not the earliest. He describes his wine as the 'Rolls Royce' of organic production, and it is certainly of high quality. A very interesting tasting clearly showed the variation in style between the years, each one producing a quite distinct character. The wines are always about 80 per cent Merlot, giving a generosity of fruit and smooth texture. Comments on some of the vintages: 1979 is brown in colour indicating that it's reached peak and is beginning to dry out, the product of a vintage of ample quantity but a little thin on fruit. For those who enjoy the rather leathery, musty type of claret which conjures up pictures of tobacco-laden, staid and elite clubs in central London on a midweek afternoon, this is the one. 1982 has a good dark colour, firm fruit and good body. The tannin will support it well. 1984 is the least impressive, with a burnt smell in the bouquet; 1985 is excellent, long in the mouth, round, makes you want to drink more and more, though still young. 1986 has a flatter bouquet, is nice and rounded, lighter than the 1985 and ready to drink earlier. If asked to pick one for value and overall quality we'd plump for the 1985. Why not try the lot and compare your view with ours?

VRT; OWC for various vintages

Château Vieux-Gabiran, Bordeaux Supérieur, 1988
C £b NP V

Another excellent wine, drinking well already, packed with ripe fruit flavours. Good length, very smooth and 'commercial' — in the best sense of the word. A real winemaker's wine.

VRT; VIN; HDR

Château Jacques Blanc, St Emilion Grand Cru, 1986
C £c NP V

Very similar to the Domaine wine from the same estate, but just a little classier, being the best vats of the vintage. Rich and full with a spicy background and considerable length of flavour.

VIN; HDR; WHI

Cuvée du Maître, Château Jacques Blanc, St Emilion Grand Cru 1986

🍷 C £d NP V

The oak-aged reserve wine from this estate, made for longer life than the equivalent vintage without the wood. A complex intriguing wine that will still benefit from keeping, the undoubted quality and fruit is as yet a little closed and undeveloped. Guard it for a while if you can and a treat should ensue in a few years' time.

VRT; WHI; OWC

Château Barrail des Graves, St Emilion 1988/89

🍷 C £c NP VE

Gérard Descrambes' St Emilion is a similar style wine to his Bordeaux but from the best sites and the best vines; the result is a touch more concentrated in flavour and bouquet. Plenty of fresh fruit here, one to keep with advantage as well.

VIN; HDR

Domaine Jacques Blanc, St Emilion 1986/8

🍷 C £c NP V

Nicely weighted overall flavour with plenty of different tastes and good length. Remains pretty approachable, and keeps the alcoholic punch of a good wine. The 1988 is more open in style than the 1986, and a little fruitier.

VIN; HDR; WHI

Vieux Château Carré, St Emilion Grand Cru 1983

C £d IND V

The full fruit bouquet gives the impression of being almost sweet. 70 per cent Merlot, the rest Cabernet Sauvignon and Cabernet Franc. The Grand Cru status means the best vines, with lower yield of grapes and higher alcohol than normal.

HFW; COW

Clos du Roy, Fronsac 1983/5

C £d IND ?

90 per cent Merlot, 10 per cent Cabernet Franc. The wines are stored for 30 months before release. The '83 is brick-red in colour, good to drink now, the '85 has a stronger, darker colour and is firm and precise.

HFW

Château la Mirandole, Première Côtes de Blaye 1979/83/86
C £d PAG V
65 per cent Merlot, the balance Malbec, Cabernet Sauvignon and
Cabernet Franc. Aged for 12 months in wooden casks, from a top
quality wine producer. The 1979 is a treasure, lots of blackcurrant
fruit and strength of flavour; the 1983 is still quite purple in colour,
indicating that it will improve and soften for some time yet; the
1986 is still a bit hard and needs time to develop.
HFW; COW

Château Meric, Graves 1986/8
C £c NP VE
There are not too many organic Graves available, and this is a true
standard bearer. Lighter than the more northerly clarets, a 'refined'
wine of some elegance. The 1988 has a soft, rich nose and open
blackcurranty flavour. Classy stuff.
VIN; HDR

Clos de la Perichère, Graves Supérieures 1986
B £c UNIA VE
A medium-bodied wine, easy drinking and well made, excellent for
lunchtimes.
WHI

Château Saint-Hilaire, Graves 1986
C £d UNIA VE
Good firm fruit beginning to soften up and present itself. A good
vintage and a well made sophisticated wine, nicely rounded and
with plenty of life, interesting layers of flavour. Cabernet and
Merlot grapes.
VRT

Château Saint-Hilaire, Graves Supérieur 1983
C £d UNIA VE
A full-bodied oak-aged wine from Gabriel Guerin, now nicely
matured and richly smooth.
WHI

Château Saint-Hilaire, Graves 1975
C £e UNIA VE
From a high quality producer, this wine is from one of the two best
vintages of the decade in this region. Marvellously smooth and

rich, with opulent fruit that cruises through the taste buds pressing the repeater button as it goes. Good structure, lingering flavour, a much more interesting way to spend your money than many a bottle of basic Champagne.

VRT

Clos la Maurasse, Graves, 1983/8
🍷 C £d UNIA VE

40 per cent Merlot, 30 per cent each Cabernet Sauvignon and Cabernet Franc. The 1988 is a young wine with a purple colour but good fruit that will open up in time. The 1983 is much more accessible. Nice delicate, smooth flavour, displaying finesse.

HFW

Château Grand Canyon, Pauillac Cru Bourgeois Supérieur, 1986
🍷 C £e UNIA V

The Medoc, where this wine is made, is generally reckoned to be the place where the world's greatest wines come from. This is the only Cru Bourgeois made organically that we know of, and the class shows through immediately in the flavour. 1985 was another good vintage and Bernard Jugla's wine is full of character, rounded and powerful in the mouth. Nice strong dark fruit bouquet. Tuck a few away for a while if the purse allows.

VRT; OWC

Château la Vallière, Lalande de Pomerol, 1983
🍾 C £d IND ?

Intense deep ruby colour, looks like the wine will go on ageing to advantage for some time yet. Bronze Medal International Wine Challenge 1989.

HFW

Château Lafleur du Roy, Pomerol, 1983
🍾 C £e IND ?

Coded to drink now, but it will last nicely for some time if you want to keep it. Well-developed bouquet of ripe fruit. A fine wine, 80 per cent Merlot, 20 per cent Cabernet Sauvignon and Cabernet Franc.

HFW

Château la Rose Haut-Musset, Lalande de Pomerol, 1987/88
🍾 C £e FESA ?

From the satellite Appellation Contrôlée region of Pomerol, home

of the world's most expensive wine, Château Petrus. The distributors describe the wine as 'already very approachable with complex jammy fruit showing through the overlay of new wood which adds an appealing vanilla freshness to both bouquet and palate'. The 1988 vintage won a Gold Medal at Bordeaux in 1989.
  VRT

Beaujolais

Beaujolais Supérieur, Château de Boisfranc 1989
A £b NP VE

Like the 1988 which you may still find available, the wine from this delightful estate with its large old Château has more body and character than many Beaujolais. Plenty of Gamay fruit, and vinified to give a bit more weight to the wine than is often the case, the slight but appealing tannin fills out the flavour nicely. Slightly earthy background, the 1989 is from a superb vintage, though unhappily there is not a large quantity available. 1990 may not appear at all as Thierry Doat used most of his grapes to make Beaujolais Nouveau; the grape harvest was especially small in 1990 due to problems with the frost killing off young buds.
  VIN; HDR; WHI

Beaujolais Nouveau, Château de Boisfranc
A £b NP VE

Crystal balls apart, we can only base each year's expected vintage on the previous ones. The wine, from a Beaujolais Supérieur producer, is usually of very high quality. It's so different from most of the conventional Nouveau in style that it can be considered untypical; normally Thierry Doat's Nouveau is more full-bodied, with greater weight, tannin and character. And always a full rich Gamay style.
  VIN; HDR

Beaujolais 1988/89, Gérard Belaid
A £c NP VE

Gamay through and through, immediate forceful flavour of the ripe fruit — nothing shy in this wine. Tastes like it smells — lovely! The difference between cheap and nasty, often acidic or flat Beaujolais lacking in fruit, and the good quality products is clearly shown here.
  VRT

Régnié Cru Classé, Christian Ducroux 1988/89
A £c NP VE

Organic since 1980, 5 hectares in total, Christian Ducroux makes first rate, delicious upfront, jammy wine from the Gamay grape. Régnié is the most recent Beaujolais area to be upgraded to Cru Classé status, and Christian's wine shows why. More character than straightforward Beaujolais.
VRT; VIN; HDR; WHI; OWC

Jean-Pierre Nesme Morgon, 1986
C £c NP VE

From one of the Cru villages of Beaujolais (ie amongst the best), this Morgon is very rich and weighty for the Gamay wines commonly associated with the area. Dark colour, strong, full flavours. Classy wine, lingers well in the mouth. Bronze Medal at the International Wine Challenge 1989.
VRT; WHI

Burgundy

Guy Chaumont, Bourgogne, 1986/7
C £c NP V

Rich Pinot Noir, long and mellow, the 1986 carries a little more weight in both colour and structure than the 1987.
VIN; HDR

D'Heilly-Huberdeau, Bourgogne Passetoutgrain 1987
B £b NP VE

Light to medium-bodied, an easy drinking fruity wine from the blend of Gamay and Pinot Noir grapes, not too dry and suitable with a wide variety of food. Try drinking it chilled on a hot summer day as an alternative to white wine.
WHI

D'Heilly-Huberdeau, Bourgogne Pinot Noir, 1988
B £c NP V

Straightforward, uncomplicated Pinot Noir. Early drinking no problem here as the style is not difficult. Plenty of interlacing flavours and nice upfront fruit. Silver Medal winner at Mâcon.
VRT; WHI

Domaine A Chaumont, Mercurey 1986
🍾 B £d UNIA ?
This is what the producer says in summary about his wine: 'Colour: red cherry. Nose: peppery, fruity. Taste: Tannic, well balanced. To drink with red meats.' Brief but accurate. Still a bit closed up, it will smoothen and develop with a few more years in the bottle. But it's excellent stuff; Mercurey is in the Côte Chalonnais, south of the more dizzy heights of the Côte d'Or. The wines can be weightier than those to the north and can be excellent value.
HFW

Domaine Javillier, Volnay-Santenots 1986
🍾 B £c/d NP ?
Volnay-Santenots is the place, or rather places — Santenots is the vineyard which lies between the villages of Volnay and Meursault. High quality wine from Pinot Noir grapes, elegant and with greater benefit to come from ageing in the bottle.
HFW; OWC

Domaine Michel Briday 1er Cru 'Champ Clou', Rully, 1986
🍾 B £d UNIA ?
Rully is the place, 'Champ Clou' the vineyard site. Premier Cru is second only to Grand Cru in the pecking order of wines from Burgundy. From Pinot Noir grapes, one that will develop further from its strong, firm base. Good deep colour.
HFW

Domaine Musso, Hautes Côtes de Beaune 1988
B £d NP V
Aromatic and slightly spicy bouquet, crystal clear colour, firm closely knit flavour. From one of the best Burgundy areas.
HFW; COW

Domaine Musso, Bourgogne Passetoutgrain 1985
B £c NP V
Passetoutgrain is the name for a blend of Gamay and Pinot Noir in the Burgundy region. This is a soft, fruity easy drinking example, fairly typical of good Passetoutgrain. Generally not as rich as 100 per cent Pinot Noir wines, and somewhat lighter, but easy and accessible.
HFW; COW

Domaine J Rateau, Clos des Mariages, Beaune 1987
◼▶ B £d NP ?

From a low yield (=higher quality) of just over 30 hectolitres per hectare, produce of a tiny half-hectare walled vineyard (1.2 acres) near Beaune. 100 per cent Pinot Noir, hand-picked grapes, aged in oak prior to release. A fine quality conscious producer, the wine has a bright ruby colour and although this was not one of the greater vintages in the region, M Rateau has produced a well integrated wine that will develop with age.

HFW

Domaine J Rateau, Côte de Beaune 'La Grande Châtelaine', 1987
B £d NP ?

Lighter than his Clos des Mariages wine, from a different and even smaller vineyard site, this is good to drink now. Similar style, light bouquet, rounded fruit and tannins.

HFW

Alain Guillot, Bourgogne Rouge 1987
B £c FNAB VE

Alain Guillot is a fervent *biologiste*. Organic since 1954, and one of the few producers to make wine without the addition of SO_2 at all. His grapes are literally untouched by any treatment or addition except for very few applications of Bordeaux Mixture in the vineyard. No fining, no filtration. The wines come from Cruzille in the Mâcon region and this red is light and easy, with a nice fruit flavour, if a little restrained in its depth. If ever in the area, visit the property and do not miss their museum with over 3000 rural artefacts from the region.

WHI

Alain Guillot, Mâcon Rouge 1988
B £c FNAB VE

From the Gamay grape, lighter than his Bourgogne Rouge, but also made with minimal disruption to the natural processes. Each bottle is sealed with a wax covering in place of the standard foil; this is a better barrier against the air, important for a wine with no added sulphur to give extra protection against possible oxidation. But it's a waiter's nightmare as the wax crumbles when the cork is pulled, and it's a skilled job to stop the flakes falling into the bottle!

WHI

Alain Verdet, Hautes Côtes de Nuits 1986
B £d/e FNAB V

From one of the very best organic winemakers in France. We tasted a whole range of his wines and scored this one 16 out of a possible 20. It is far better than the 1987 vintage which follows, not that there is anything wrong with that. Rich in colour and taste, beautifully rounded flavour which lingers in the mouth. An elegant wine from the Pinot Noir grape, smooth and silky. Alain Verdet has been making wine organically since 1970 and currently has 8 hectares, with another 7 to come on stream. He originally had a demand from customers for organically-grown fruits such as pears, and on taking over the vineyard from his father, converted to organic methods. Alain studied with M Lemaire, one of the founding fathers of the organic movement in France, and the Lemaire part of the now superseded Lemaire-Boucher organization. He says that organic is not simply good environmentally, but also produces higher quality fruit. This, combined with his particular vineyard site and soil, enable him to make wines of a quality which are several grades above their official appellation status. SO_2 is added in small quantities during fermentation, but is all 'eaten up' during the process. Further SO_2 is added prior to bottling, leaving a residual amount of approximately 15–20 mg per litre. Quantities harvested are quite low, with a maximum of 40–45 hectolitres per hectare. In 1988 and '89 the harvest was only 25 hectos/hectare. Oak ageing is usually at least 18 months for the 'normal' wines and 2 years for the 'Fût Neuf' (new oak). He speaks very highly of the 1989 vintage, indicating that it will be tannic and long-lasting before eventually becoming one of the great wines of the decade. Apparently many growers had a problem with the vintage lacking acidity, necessitating the addition of tartaric acid to give the wine some bite. In his case the long period of vinification helped to extract the acids and tannin from the grapes, giving the wine sufficient natural bite. We look forward with interest to the release of the wine in a few years' time.

VRT; HFW; VIN; HDR; WHI

Alain Verdet, Hautes Côtes de Nuits 1982, 1987
B £d FNAB V

Different vintages from the Burgundian master; the 1982 is ageing nicely now, browning slightly at the edges, with a delicious texture and ripe flavour. The 1987 is quite different in character, light, still

young in colour, and while delightfully fruity it is from a vintage that lacks the concentration of flavour of earlier years.
OWC

Alain Verdet Hautes Côtes de Nuits 'Fût Neuf' 1982/6/7
▷ B £d/e FNAB V
This selection of 4 vintages are all wines that have been aged for 12 months in small new oak barrels before bottling. The effect of this is to infuse the wine's own fruit flavour with the oakiness of the wood, along with a stiffening belt of additional tannin. The wines that result thus have greater ageing potential, and all of these can be kept with advantage. These are very fine wines, regularly winning awards at competitions. The 1982 is opening up and has full soft flavours; the 1986 is still a little closed but has lovely rich fruit flavours, which will open out further making this a velvety, aristocratic wine; 1987 is younger and substantially lighter than the '86. With a fabulous bouquet, it will evolve with further time in the bottle, and is warm, smooth and round. The difference between this oak-aged wine and the same vintage which has not had the treatment is a lesson in itself — the oak-aged version is a wine of greater stature. Not that the basic edition is bad!
OWC; VRT and HFW(1986 only)

Alain Verdet, Pinot Noir, Bourgogne 1988
B £c FNAB V
The quality categories in this region start with the general level of Burgundy (Bourgogne), so this is a wine from the simplest level. But coming from this excellent producer it will probably surprise with its quality, warmly rounded and smooth, good structure, but lighter and less concentrated than his Hautes Côtes de Nuits wines. Good value.
OWC

Languedoc and Roussillon
Albaric, Vin de Pays du Gard
B £a NP VE
A wine that comes from the 'Bouches du Rhône' region, though not with that designation in the title. The Bouches du Rhône is, literally, the mouth of the Rhône river, where it flows into the sea. This wine is from a blend of local grape varieties producing a spicy, cinnamon flavoured medium to full-bodied wine. Well priced and

fairly distinctive, it has been matured in Russian oak casks made in the time of the Czars.

VRT; OWC; BUP

Bishop's Wine, Vin de Pays du Gard
B £b NP VE

What can we say — the organic answer to 'Glühwein'. This is a bottle of Albaric Vin de Pays with a sachet of herbs and spices, complete with instructions, ready to knock up a mulled wine at the drop of a hat.

OWC

Château de Caraguilhes, Corbières 1986/88/89
D £b UNIA V

A dark, rich colour with a ripe bouquet. Loads of fruit, rich peppery flavours, and good length. This estate consistently makes good wines of excellent value. They recently joined UNIA after being independent. To our knowledge this is the largest single verified organic estate, with 130 hectares producing half a million bottles a year, 75 per cent of it red. This wine is based on a blend of Carignan, Grenache, Cinsault and Syrah grapes

SAF(88); VRT(89); HFW; COW; TES(88)

Château de Caraguilhes, Corbières 1983
D £b IND V

Smokey bouquet, deep rich colour, and a blackcurranty style that lasts in the mouth. Well made stuff.

HFW; COW

Château de Caraguilhes, Corbières 1979
D £c IND ?

Having had time to age, the wine has mellowed out but retains good balance and is a lively mouthful. Like other vintages it lasts well and has nicely integrated flavours.

HFW

Château St Jean d'Aumières, Coteaux de Languedoc, 1986
C £b IND V

Syrah, Grenache, Cinsault and Carignan grapes, from a small (4 hectare) estate run by Daniel Delclaud and his wife. The Syrah flavour is predominant in this wine — a warm, rubbery character

— quite spicy and with good fruit. A big wine, nice with cheese. Good value.
 HFW; COW

Clos St Martin, Vin de Pays de Pyrenées Orientales, 1989
 C £b NP ?
Carignan, Cinsault and other local grape varieties make up this medium, fruity and accessible red. With a light aromatic bouquet, it is clean and straightforward.
 HFW

Côtes du Jura Trousseau 1986, Michel Terrier
 C £c FESA VE
A little-known region and a little-known grape. The Jura region is in the very east of France, and is best known for its white wines, although these are quite hard to come by in the UK. The Trousseau grape which produces this red wine is a rogue inhabitant of a very small area of the Jura; it is unknown elsewhere in France but, under different synonyms, appears in several guises around the world, most notably as the wonderfully named Bastardo grape in Portugal where it is blended in the production of Port. It can make rich, full-bodied wines in the Jura. This one should keep for several years yet.
 WHI

Côtes du Roussillon, Coronat 1988
 C £b NP V
Gutsy and rustic, a biggish wine from the south. Dark heavy fruit, powerful, forward flavour. Drink it with food.
 VRT; SED

Simone Couderc, Coteaux du Languedoc, 1987
 E £b NP VE
This is a fabulous wine but one to be wary of! It is extraordinarily dark, rich, tannic and weighty. A viniferous equivalent to Marmite — stick a knife and fork in and you might expect it to stand up! It is super-organic, being made from the best hand-picked grapes where the whole bunches are fermented unpressed, extracting maximum flavour and, in this case, tannin. The wine has no SO_2 added, the bottles have plenty of deposit in them (natural and harmless) and the wine is unique in character. It will improve, soften and mellow for years; if drinking now, be sure to do so

with a strongly flavoured meal. Syrah, Carignan, Grenache.
VIN; HDR; WHI; EDB

Domaine de L'Ametlier, Vin de Pays de Pezenas
C £b NP V

A good little wine, a bit unkempt at the edges in true country style, but with plenty of chocolatey character to see that off. Pezenas is the town of Molière in the south of France, also famous for its connections with Clive of India. Charlie Regol is the name of the proprietor, and despite his name there is nothing English about him at all. He did not actually make wine until 1987, previously growing grapes to eat. This wine is dark blackish red in colour, with liquorice overtones, rich and strong in flavour. We enjoyed it best of all with food.
HDR; VIN

Domaine Anthea Merlot, Vin de Pays d'Oc, 1990
C £b UNIA ?

An earlier vintage of this wine was selected by Charles Metcalfe in *Wine Magazine* as his Red Wine of the Month and described as 'the Petrus of the Midi'. High praise indeed; the predominance of the Merlot grape's plummy, warm, mellow and appetizing flavour is what makes this so appealing.
SAF

Domaine de Bargac, Vin de Pays du Gard, 1989
B £a UNIA VE

Delightful wine with vivid, fresh, light cherry-fruit flavour. Excellent value from Southern France and made to highlight the freshness and vivacity of the grapes. Medium-bodied.
ASD

Domaine Belles Croix Robin, Vin de Pays du Val de Montferrand, 1988
B £b NP ?

Merlot, Grenache, Carignan and Cabernet grapes. A good all-round wine, decent fruit and flavour. Pleasantly earthy.
HFW

Domaine de la Bousquette, Saint Chinian 1988
B £b NP V

Carignan, Grenache and Cinsault grapes, robust, but a little flat, with the tannin still blocking the fruit flavour. Not a bad wine, but rather straightforward and monodimensional.

VRT

Domaine Bosquet-Canet Cabernet Sauvignon, Vin de Pays des Sables du Golfe du Lion, 1988
B £b IND V

With low sulphur content, the wine has a medium-bodied, supple flavour and aromatic, lively bouquet. Made in forward style for drinking early, it is delightfully fruity and easy. Produced by the giant Listel company in the Camargue.

ABT; EDB

Domaine de Clairac Joubio, Vin de Pays de L'Hérault
B £b UNIA V

We have given this a rating for drinking now, but the wine has considerable tannin to back up the fruit. This region can produce very earthy wines, perhaps a little coarse or rough and ready, but not detrimentally so. There is lots of good fruit and if left for a few hours the wine really opens up. Excellent everyday value.

HDR; VIN; CRS

Domaine de Clairac Cabernet, Vin de Pays de L'Hérault
B £b UNIA ?

Cabernet Franc grapes from the south of France, aged in oak prior to bottling. Strong, full-bodied, slightly stalky flavour. Best with food.

SED

Domaine de Clairac Jougla, Vin de Table
B £a UNIA V

Quite jammy, full-bodied and robust, plenty of fruit and sometimes a healthy dose of tannin. Comes in both 75cl and 100cl bottles. A blend of southern grape varieties, with a solid earthy twang.

VIN; HDR

Domaine de Clairac Syrah, Vin de Pays de L'Hérault, 1988
C £b UNIA V

Classic Syrah, rubbery bouquet, medium to full-bodied, warm, fruity and rich. No need to keep this one: it can be drunk with confidence. Youthful colour, the fresh fruit comes through nicely in the taste.
HDR; VIN

Domaine de Clairac Syrah, Vin de Pays de L'Hérault, 1986
◀▣ C £b UNIA V
Pretty robust stuff, loads of tannin. A limited production of this Gold Medal-winning wine might mean you have to search for it; essentially similar to later vintages but vinified for maximum flavour and tannin, making it one to keep for a few years yet so that it can smoothen out. For drinking now, buy the younger vintages. For a treat, keep a few bottles of this.
HDR; VIN; SED

Domaine de Farlet, Vin de Pays des Collines de la Moure, 1988
C £b NP VE
An everyday wine with a spicy cinnamon flavour, very direct and with plentiful fruit while also quite steely in character. Better with food than on its own, a reliable wine from traditional southern French grape varieties.
VRT; HDR; VIN; OWC

Domaine de Farlet Merlot, Vin de Pays des Collines de la Moure, 1988
B £b NP VE
Pretty classic southern French Merlot, plummy colour and character, very easy drinking. Fresh, juicy flavour, nicely balanced, friendly and fruity. Good value and of very general appeal — the most easy drinking wine from André Duplan's estate.
VRT; HDR; VIN; OWC;BLA

Domaine de Farlet, Vin de Pays des Collines de la Moure, Fûts de Chêne, 1985
▣▶ B £b NP VE
The oak-aged version of André Duplan's Domaine de Farlet red, the wine has added depth of character and is definitely made more 'serious' by this ageing process. Two years in oak casks give it a darker colour and rich, oaky bouquet. At this price level a wine worth trying if you enjoy the weighty style.
OWC

Domaine Aimé Fontanel, Fitou 1987
D £b IND V

A deep dark ruby colour from 70 per cent Carignan and 30 per cent Grenache and Syrah, aged for 18 months. An aggressive mixture of solid fruits and tannins producing an interesting single estate Fitou.
HFW; COW

Domaine du Grand Bourry, Costières de Nîmes, 1989
C £b NP No

Spicy dark fruit flavours from the south, a blend based on Cabernet Sauvignon and including local varieties. Richly complex, benefiting from oak ageing, very good value.
VRT

Domaine St Jean d'Aumières Cabernet, Vin de Pays de Gorges de L'Hérault, 1986
C £b IND ?

100 per cent Cabernet Sauvignon, 12 months' storage in old oak before bottling, from a specific area within the larger Hérault region. Fine, deep, rich flavour and original varietal character.
HFW

Domaine St Jean d'Aumières, Coteaux de Languedoc, 1986
C £b IND ?

As for the Château wine, but from vines grown in a less favourable site and thus producing a wine slightly less pronounced in all respects — a little less fruity and concentrated, but essentially the same. Sufficient tannin to age, well made and with good lingering flavour.
HFW

Domaine de L'Ile Cabernet, Vin de Pays de L'Aude 1988
B £b UNIA VE

Deep garnet in colour with tinges of youthful purple, a soft but full-bodied wine with concentrated blackcurrant flavour. M Bissa is a 'returnee', having left the world of television technology to tend organic vines. His property of 18 hectares produces reds and whites, labelled either as Domaine de L'Ile or Château Caderonne: it's all the same place! The Cabernet, like his whites, is down to earth and immediate in style, much better than its Vin de Pays status. Rustic, with excellent fruit character.
VRT

Domaine de Malaric, Vin de Pays de l'Uzège
B £b UNIA ?

Rich purple colour and deep plummy bouquet. Quite an unusual, distinctive wine which might well improve with a bit of keeping. Full southern style.
OWC

Domaine de Picheral Merlot/Syrah, Vin de Pays d'Oc, 1989
C £a NP V

Extraordinary good value, a marvellously well made wine from the south. Merlot and Syrah is an enticing combination and the balance creates a delicious, mellow mouthful. Gold Medal Winner.
WMO

Domaine de Picheral Rouge, Vin de Pays d'Oc, 1989
B £b NP V

Nice, spicy, slightly peppery flavour to this medium-bodied wine from a blend of grapes including Carignan, Cinsault and Syrah.
SAF

Domaine de Picheral Syrah, Vin de Pays d'Oc, 1989
C £b NP V

100 per cent Syrah grape, an extraordinarily full, rich wine, showing the weight and character of this grape variety in textbook style. Very distinctive, almost loud in flavour, unmistakably Syrah.
SAF

Domaine des Soulié, Saint Chinian, 1988/9
B £b UNIA VE

From Syrah, Grenache, Mourvedre and Cinsault grapes, a marvellous, earthy wine, full of southern fruit. Plummy, refreshingly honest fruit balanced by good backbone makes this an excellent example of the high quality now being achieved in parts of southern France.
ABT

Guige et fils, Vin du Pays des Coteaux de Cèze
C £b FESA VE

We have not been able to taste this wine, and the distributors' notes simply say 'A round aromatic wine. Excellent value'. We can but hope things will evolve . . .
WHI

L'Olivier, Vin de Pays de L'Hérault 1988/89
B £b NP VE

André Duplan makes three Vin de Pays wines at his estate. The Olivier is from traditional grape varieties and carries the Vin de Pays de L'Hérault designation. The other wines are not Hérault, but Collines de la Moure. The latter is a subsection within the Hérault, and requires a minimum alcohol level of 11 per cent against 10 per cent for the Hérault, and a maximum yield of 70 hectolitres per hectare as against 80 for the Hérault. M Duplan's estate is well-situated for organic wine production in a self-contained area protected by trees, the sea breeze and the heat. This wine has a youthful colour and nice spicy bouquet of cinnamon and cloves, making a pleasant medium-bodied glassful.

HDR; VIN

Lou Pas D'Estrech, Vin de Pays des Coteaux de Cèze, 1989
B £b UNIA ?

From the Gard region — Coteaux de Cèze is north of Avignon. This is a nice, open, lunchtime-type wine. Good rounded flavour of light red fruit in the mouth, bit of spice and jammy enough to make it good for drinking on its own as well as with food.

VRT

Mas de Daumas Gassac, 1988
D £d IND V

This estate is rapidly becoming something of a legend. Although only classified as a table wine because of their use of non-approved grape varieties — notably Cabernet Sauvignon — this is quite superb. Made in the Hérault region, an extraordinary wine, heralded in the press world wide over many vintages, the character is of big, integrated, long-lasting reds in the style of the great clarets. If starting a mini-cellar, put this one top of the list. The 1988 is a long way off its peak, being an extraordinary purple colour and still very closed up — the fullness of the fruit character has yet to be revealed. Silver Medal, International Wine Challenge 1990.

VRT; ODD

La Sarabande Vin de Pays du Gard
B £b FESA ?

Another of the southern French everyday drinkers. Medium to full-bodied, uncomplicated, with a nice spicy nose and deepish red colour.

OWC

'*Le Taureau Noir*', *Vin de Pays du Gard*
B £b NP ?

A straightforward, simple country wine for everyday quaffing. For drinking young with some fruit in the flavour and spice in the bouquet.
OWC

Safeway Organic Vin de Table
B £a UNIA V

One of the few really good wines to retail at under £3 a bottle. Described in *Which? Wine Monthly* as having 'juicy ripe fruit on the nose, and a soft and spicy palate balanced by enough acidity to make this a clean, thirst quenching wine for current drinking'.
SAF

Vin de Pays des Pyrénées Orientales, Coronat
B £b NP ?

A light ruby-coloured wine from the Roussillon. Fully fruity bouquet, the flavour of blackberries in the mouth.
VRT

Loire

Anjou Rouge, Domaine de Dreuillé 1988/89
A £b EAP VE

Terrific wine, bags of rich raspberry fruit, smooth and silky, a real example of how Loire reds can match the more popular whites. Predominantly Cabernet Franc. The 1989 won a Silver Medal at Mâcon.
VRT

Anjou Rouge, Gérard Leroux, 1983/5/6/8
B £b NP V

Organic wines are sometimes said to be more uncomplicated, earthy, possibly more straightforward, individual and immediate in style. This is a case in point. These wines have plenty of fruit and nice tannin to give weight and background. Made from Cabernet Franc grapes, they are slightly rustic, more in the frame of the country kitchen than the fitted units of darkest Surrey. With a weightier style than many Anjou reds, they keep well.
VIN; HDR; WHI

Gamay, Vin de Pays du Jardin de la France, Domaine de la Parentière 1989
A £b NP VE

Fresh and fruity, with the flavours of ripe berries. Vibrant in colour, it has the typical boiled sweets character associated with the Gamay grape. Light-bodied and 'more-ish'.
VRT

Vin de Pays des Marches de Bretagne, Cabernet, Bossard
B £b FESA VE

It would be surprising if this extraordinary winemaker produced anything other than an exceptional wine. His whites have received accolades on many different occasions, over many different vintages. This red is clearly from the same stable; excellent chewy ripe fruit, medium-bodied, its easy to see what is meant when people say a wine is alive. The wine is not fined at all, being left over the winter to settle naturally. Cabernet Franc grapes. *Wine Magazine* Red Wine of the Month September 1990.
VRT; VIN; HDR

Bourgueil, J Guion 1985
B £c UNIA ?

100 per cent Cabernet Franc, from M Guion's small vineyard. Stored in oak barrels for 18 months prior to being released. Deep red colour, weighty for Bourgeuil, with a smell of cherries in the bouquet. Rich, nicely textured wine.
HFW

Gamay Rouge, VDQS, Coteaux du Giennois, Alain Paulet 1987
B £c NP ?

Pure Gamay grape. Fermentation starts off with the whole berries in a traditional open vat before being transferred to stainless steel for further fermentation. Subsequently oak-aged for 4–8 months, the wine has a clear bright ruby colour and is full and smooth in the mouth.
HFW

Sancerre Red 1989, Christian et Nicole Dauny
A £c FESA V

The only Sancerre producer that we know of to make wine according to organic methods, the Daunys' wines vary considerably from vintage to vintage. Not that they are ever bad, but the character changes quite a lot and at the price being asked for Sancerre these days, we are entitled to value for money. This vintage of the red, made from Pinot Noir, is light but with a hint of body in the flavour. When first tasted early in the year it seemed dull and very flat. Six months later it appeared to have gained in character enormously and to be mellow, lively and nicely balanced.

GJF

Saumur-Champigny, Clos Rougeard 1986
B £d NP ?

Another Cabernet Franc grape from the Loire valley, but here a rather special candidate. From 30-year-old vines, the wine has been aged for 2 years in oak barrels from the famous Château Margaux. Quality, not quantity, is the watchword and the end result is terrific. Full, developed colour, overladen oaky taste but with highly concentrated fruit flavour. Hand crafted and individual, of limited quantity.

HFW; COW

Pinot Noir Rouge, VDQS, Coteaux du Giennois 1987
B £c NP ?

From the central Loire valley, in the region that gives us Pouilly-Fumé, this red is uniquely Pinot Noir grapes. The northern climate has produced a finely balanced wine with ripe acidity and soft fruit flavours.

HFW

Provence

Château Barbeyrolles, Côtes de Provence, 1986
D £c IND ?

80 per cent Grenache, Syrah and Mourvedre, 20 per cent Cabernet Sauvignon and Cinsault. The grapes are vinified separately before blending to ensure an appropriate selection each year, and the resulting wine is stored in oak for 15–18 months prior to release. This has a deep ruby colour and complex range of flavours. It will develop if kept.

HFW

Château Vignelaure, Coteaux d'Aix-en-Provence, 1985
C £d FESA ?

One of the clutch of top-rate Provençal estates to feature in this

guide, the estate had just been taken over by new owners at the time of writing. Near Aix-en-Provence, it is in the same league as the Domaine Richeaume wines. The 1985 vintage is big, full and powerful, but still retaining plenty of finesse.
HFW

Rouge d'Eté, Côtes de Provence, 1989
C £b IND ?

Full red colour with a spicy edge. From Syrah, Mourvedre and Cabernet Sauvignon. As its name suggests it is made as a young, jolly wine to wallop down with whatever is at hand. From Régine and Roger Sumeire's Château La Tour de L'Eveque.
HFW

Domaine du Jas D'Esclans Cru Classé, 1986
D £b IND V

Silver Medal, International Wine Challenge 1990. From René Lorgues' Cru Classé estate of 53 hectares — large by organic standards, a smooth, tarry, robust wine of excellent value, being significantly cheaper than some of the other estates in this area. Made from 50 per cent Cinsault, 25 per cent Grenache, 15 per cent Mourvedre and 10 per cent Syrah, the wine is aged in large oak barrels for 2–3 years before being released. An excellent smooth wine, good with strong foods.
VIN; HDR; HFW; EDB

Domaine Saint-Cyriaque, Coteaux Varios VDQS 1988
C £b NP VE

We have tasted this wine on several occasions and just cannot work up much enthusiasm. While pleasant enough, it is unexceptional, a bit flat and thin. Made as a light easy drinking wine, it serves well enough for this purpose.
OWC; GJF

Domaine Saint-Cyriaque, Coteaux Varios VDQS, 'Cuvée Spéciale' 1987
D £b NP VE

The pick of the crop from Claude Courtois, deep garnet red colour and Rhône-style bouquet. From Grenache and Syrah, aged in oak for 12 months; fresh, warm taste. The myriad of different flavours produces a rich, complex wine.
OWC; GJF

Domaine Richeaume Cabernet Sauvignon, 1988

▄▆► D £d FESA V

'Bloody marvellous' was the response of one northern merchant. Kathryn McWhirter in the *Independent on Sunday*, August 1990, seemed to agree, selecting it as the best red in a tasting of some 75 organic wines. Hoening Hoesch is a Yale-educated German who bought land in the foothills of the Mont Sainte-Victoire and planted 25 hectares of vines, as well as a variety of other crops including wheat and vegetables. The first vintage was in 1975 and the emphasis is firmly on quality as evidenced by the restricted output, which at around 35 hectolitres per hectare is small (only 25 in 1989 — watch the prices!). His cellar resembles a gallery as much as a winery, beautifully designed and decorated with works of art. This is all part of the attitude that integrates the practical and the aesthetic, work and philosophy. The Cabernet Sauvignon is aged in small oak barrels (new and less so) for 5 to 10 months and the wine is exceptional — still a bit rough at the edges and quite bitingly tannic, but overflowing with deep Cabernet character and packed with fruit. 'Supervin'.

VIN; HDR

Domaine Richeaume Syrah 1988

▄▆► D £d FESA V

As for the Cabenet Sauvignon, from the same glorious vintage, but 100 per cent Syrah grape. Hoening Hoesch makes a much smaller quantity of Syrah. It is more immediately accessible in style, a ripe luscious mouthful to accompany bold foods.

VIN; HDR

▌ *Domaine Richeaume, Cuvée Tradition 1987*
▐ C £c FESA V

A blend of Grenache, Cinsault, Carignan and Cabernet Sauvignon. The Cabernet gives it breadth of character and firmness of structure. Now opening up into a lovely smooth rich red, delightful bouquet. Warm, easy and a fascinating contrast to the single grape variety wines.

VIN; HDR

▐ *Mas de la Dame, Coteaux D'Aix-en-Provence, Les Baux, 1987/88*
▐ C £b IND V

A blend of Grenache, Cabernet Sauvignon and Syrah, aged in old oak barrels for 12 months prior to bottling. Low final sulphur levels — 10mg/litre — and a smooth, rich character make this a fine, good value introduction to the small and high quality region of Les Baux. Ripe, earthy flavour.

ABT

Mas de Gourgonnier Tradition Coteaux d'Aix-en-Provence, Les Baux, 1989

🍾 D £b NP V

Different from the réserve wine below in that it is vinified for earlier drinking; the vintage seems to lend itself to this as well. Soft, fruity nose and full, approachable flavour. While it will no doubt improve with keeping (hence our coding) it is also drinking well now.

HFW; COW

Mas de Gourgonnier Coteaux d'Aix-en-Provence, Les Baux, Réserve du Mas 1983/6

🍾 D £d NP ?

Two vintages of the réserve wine from this super estate, one of the new breed of Provençal producers experimenting with grape varieties and styles. From the area around the village of Baux at the foothills of the small 'Les Alpilles' mountain range, the vines are grown on chalky soil high in mineral content. Some of the most exciting wines are currently coming from the quality-conscious organic estates in this region and Mas de Gourgonnier is one of them. 45 per cent Cabernet Sauvignon, blended with Syrah and Mourvedre, from selected best grapes will make powerful, rich, full-bodied wines with a deep ruby colour. The 1983 is drinking nicely, the 1986 will benefit from further ageing as the flavours have not yet opened up as much as they will do. Top quality winemaking.

HFW; OWC

Terres Blanches, Coteaux d'Aix-en-Provence, Les Baux, 1988

🍾 D £c FESA V

50 per cent Grenache, the rest Cinsault and Counoise. Really big chunky red wines are made here (as well as rosé and white). The 1988 has a deep rich purple colour at present and a supple, fruit flavour, with lots of weight and chocolatey overtones in the taste. A top quality estate making wines with real individuality and flair.

WCL

Rhône

Cave la Vigneronne Villedieu, Côtes du Rhône 1989
◼▶ C £b NP VE

This wine is made at the excellent Co-operative at Villedieu from grapes grown by four different growers, all adhering to Nature et Progrès regulations. Because all the other wines made here are not based on organic grapes, scrupulous care is taken to ensure that the whole process is carried out in clean and separate presses and vats. The style of wine makes an interesting contrast to the other Côtes du Rhône available, being made for early or medium term drinking, without lots of tannin and with bags of juicy fruit. Medium-bodied and succulent, lightly spicy background flavours.

VIN; HDR; WHI; OWC

Domaine St Apollinare, Côtes du Rhône, Cuvée d'Apolline 1987/88
◼▶ C £b IND/DYN No

A biodynamic wine, medium to full-bodied, warm and still with considerable tannin. A multitude of different flavours: cedar, cloves, nutmeg, liquorice to name a few. Not a middle ground wine — it's too definite and forthright. Bags of character, from Grenache, Cinsault and Syrah. M Daumas' publicity says 'Every amateur enthusiast of good wines should have one in their cellar'. He has his own particular trademark for organic production, DYNORGA. Bronze Medal at the International Wine Challenge 1990.

VRT; OWC; SAN

Domaine Saint Apollinaire, Côtes du Rhône, 'Cuvée de Cépage Syrah', 1987/88
◼▶ C £b IND/DYN No

An extraordinary individual and unusual wine with a multitude of rich, spicy flavours, dark purple in colour, and very tannic. Warm, muddy fruit and rubbery Syrah character; a wine for those who want to explore the diversity of styles, not for quaffing. A fascinating wine that will improve and soften with age.

OWC(87)

Pierre Perrin, Côtes du Rhône
◧ C £c IND ?

Well made and nicely rounded, a rich and quite traditional style Côtes du Rhône. Good peppery background character. Best with food.

BUP

Vignoble de la Jasse, Côtes du Rhône, 1988/9
C £b NP VE

Daniel Combe does just about everything himself in his vineyard, divided between two sites in the small town of Violes. His wine is of delightfully high standard from year to year, and is another example of the high quality that exists among the organic growers in the Rhône. This wine has the depth of character of a Gigondas or Vacqueras, with a lovely spicy flavour, and closely knitted structure but displaying wildly rich fruits. Made by a super-organic producer, just a hint of residual sulphur, no fining, no filtration, simply left to become clear by natural decanting over the winter months. The total area is 10 hectares, and he deliberately keeps the quantity down to 30 hectolitres/hectare, so increasing the quality of the grape. Commended at the International Wine Challenge 1990.

VIN; HDR; CRS; ODD

Domaine de L'Attilon Cabernet Sauvignon, Vin de Pays des Bouches du Rhône 1988/9
C £b NP VE

A firm structure, with a bit of grip in the flavour. Straight Cabernet Sauvignon, good integrated fruit with blackcurrant overtones. The wines are best after about a year.

VIN; HDR

Domaine de L'Attilon Merlot, Vin de Pays des Bouches du Rhône 1988/9
B £b NP VE

Fairly characteristic of the Merlot grape, plummy flavour with the distinctive mellow puffiness that always conjures up associations with marshmallows! Medium-bodied and fruity, pretty straight-forward and none the worse for that.

HDR; VIN; MWW

Domaine de Beaujeu, Vin de Pays des Bouches du Rhône 1989
C £b NP V

From Nicolas Cartier who also owns the Provençal Mas de Gourgonnier, an interesting fragrant wine from his second property. Easy drinking and with good depth, from Carignan, Syrah, Cinsault and Mourvedre grapes.

HFW; COW; OWC

Domaine Gautières, Vin de Pays des Coteaux des Baronnies, 1988
C £b NP ?

45 per cent Syrah, the balance from Grenache, Mourvedre and
Cinsault. The grapes are not pressed before vinification, being
placed whole into the vat. The Syrah is predominant in the
character and flavour as you would expect, but plenty of other fruits
are evident too. An interesting mix and good value.
HFW

Domaine St Apollinaire, Dynorga
C £b IND/DYN No

The everyday drinking wine from M Daumas is made from a variety
of grape types and is light in colour, not too alcoholic and with a
light bouquet that he describes as being like Muscat.
VRT

Pierre André, Châteauneuf-du-Pape, 1986/8
D £d FESA V

An excellent peppery wine from a blend of Grenache, Syrah,
Mourvedre and Cinsault, with small amounts of other varieties.
The wine is oak-aged for at least a year before bottling. Fining is
with organic egg whites. Low yields and high quality from a small
property run by Pierre and his daughter Jacqueline. A dark rich
colour, replicated in the flavour, firm and yet smooth. The wine is
not filtered as this is felt to remove some of the flavour; there may
be a light deposit, but the wine is quite clear. The 1986 is still more
closed than the very upfront 1988, and needs opening at least three
hours before drinking. Diploma of Honour at Concours de
Dégustation in Châteauneuf-du-Pape 1987.
VRT; VIN; HDR

Château de Beaucastel, Châteauneuf-du-Pape, 1981/6/7
D £ef IND V

Pierre Perrin's wine has trail-blazed for organic methods. It is of
such undoubtedly high quality that it is impossible not to
recognize the benefit of good grapes and good winemaking.
Various vintages are available from many different sources around
the country. Châteauneuf-du-Pape allows 13 different grapes to be
used, and they are all in this wine — separately vinified before the
complex and critical blending takes place. The character of these
wines is the epitome of Châteauneuf — dark, rich, spicy and with
plenty of peppery fruit, while at the same time rounded and

smooth. The older wine is drinking well, the younger 1986 is also delightful but can be kept with advantage. The 1987 has an excellent bouquet, is packed with fruit so that it seems almost sweet, and is already smooth. 'Absolutely great' was our summary at tasting.

HFW; COW(86); ODD(87)

Crozes-Hermitage, Albert Begot, 1983/5/6
☛ C £c UNIA V

A small 5-hectare estate now run by Madame Begot producing wine with so much fruit it tastes almost sweet — it isn't of course, it's just alive and juicy, like an overripe grape. 100 per cent Syrah grapes, 3 years in oak barrels prior to bottling. The 1983 is hard to come by now, and is approaching maturity; the 1985 is probably the best of the three years, and is now ready to drink but will go on for another ten; the 1986 may mature a little earlier, and is a touch lighter than the 1985. Overall a marvellous little property whose wines are unlikely not to please. Organic since 1970. A special Cuvée is planned for the 1988, aged in new oak.

HDR; VIN (85 & 86); VRT(86); HFW(83)

Clos de l'Arbalastrier, St Joseph, 1985
☛ D £d IND ?

A massive wine, 100 per cent Syrah, plenty of different fruit flavours, from blackcurrant to violets. The vinification and storing are all in wood, the ageing being for three years prior to bottling. A well made wine which lingers long in the mouth — one taster referred to it as very 'serious'.

HFW

South West

▌ Bergerac, Selection Claire Vallée 1988
▍ C £b FESA ?

'Claire Vallée' is the marketing arm of the FESA organization, and this wine does not declare the actual producer on the label. The importers describe it as light, bright and with fresh red curranty fruit. They recommend it as picnic wine.

OWC

Château Bovila, Cahors, 1986
☛ D £b IND V

Predominantly Auxerrois grape, a big beefy chunk from southern

France. The grapes are hand-picked, the wine is fined with egg whites but not filtered. Aged in oak for 6 to 9 months before bottling, a strong, full rich wine that can be kept with advantage to mature for many years to come.
HFW

Château Laroque, Bergerac 1988
C £b FESA V

With a fresh ripe bouquet, and straightforward, clean fruity flavour, this is an amiable and easy wine.
VRT

Château Le Barradis, Bergerac Rouge 1986/8
C £b NP VE

From an estate that is best known for its sweet Monbazillac, the red has a slightly peppery bouquet, with plenty of fruit, which doesn't really carry through to the flavour. With a nice dark colour, the wine is medium to full-bodied.
VIN; HDR; WHI

Jean Guiraud, Bergerac Rouge, 1985
C £b UNIA V

A producer who was following the independent path until 1985 when he joined the Lemaire-Boucher (now UNIA) organization. Red Bergerac can all too often be a little uninspiring, but this has an appealing ease about it, medium-bodied, and with generous fruit flavours.
VRT; SED

Domaine Monbouché, Côtes de Bergerac Rouge 1988
C £b UNIA ?

Predominantly Merlot with some Cabernet Franc and Sauvignon, a medium-bodied fruity open wine, accessible and unpretentious.
HFW

ITALY

Barbera d'Asti DOC, Fratelli Rovero 1987
C £b IND ?

Barbera is the grape, Asti the place, (known best for the light and sparkling Asti Spumante), and we are in Piemonte, north west

Italy, bordering on south eastern France. This is rich on the nose and in colour, with a spicy plummy flavour and still soft and smooth. Recommended with food.
VRT

Barbera d'Asti DOC, Renato Rabezzana 1988
C £d SS VE
Aged in *barriques* (small oak casks), this is a rich full-bodied and fruity wine from Barbera grapes, one of the most widely-planted red varieties. The oak is not too dominant, knitting nicely with the grape flavours. From specially selected grapes, only a small quantity is produced.
ORG

Bardolino DOC Classico Superiore, Guerrieri-Rizzardi, 1987/88
B £b/c IND VE
From the Veneto region centred on Verona in north east Italy, the land of Soave and Valpolicella also makes the very easy drinking Bardolino. Light, cherry-like, fresh and with soft fruity character.
VRT(88); HFW; COW

Cabernet del Veneto, Zanette, 1988/89
C £b AIAB VE
A sturdy, robust flavoured wine. The 1988 vintage won a Commendation at the 1990 International Wine Challenge and is heavier than the 1989. The thing that really stands out is the pungent bouquet, and the good fruit in the flavour. However, it is not very typical of the Cabernet Sauvignon grape.
ORG

Chianti 'Villa Angiolina' DOCG, Villa Angiolina 1988
B £b SS VE
Very strong Sangiovese bouquet — almost too strong — a generally similar style of wine to their Bacco but lighter and without quite as much harmony in the flavour. Light to medium-bodied, with a warm, open style. The addition of 3–5 per cent Cabernet grapes gives a touch of added spice.
ORG; VRT

Chianti 'Bacco' DOCG, Villa Angiolina 1985/7
B £b SS VE
Actually in the Chianti Putto area but more Classico in style, they

do not want to make a light wine, prefering the more robust and traditional variety. Aged for at least 18 months before bottling, it is predominantly Sangiovese grapes with additions from three other varieties. Medium-bodied with nice background tannin adding a bit of bite to the flavour, which is quite mellow. The 1985 vintage has a stronger bouquet and slight caramelly flavour. Both have a pleasant slight petillance, the result of the 'Governo' method of adding a little unfermented grape must to the wine. These are people following very traditional styles and methods.
ORG

Chianti DOCG, Tenuta San Vito Roberto Drighi, 1988/89
B £b SS VE

The principal wine from Roberto Drighi is made from the Tuscan blend of Sangiovese, Canaiolo and Trebbiano grapes and is deliciously light and fruity, made to drink young. A very summery wine, with a slight spritz reminiscent of good Muscadet, this adds to the zesty, cherry-like style. From a Chianti Putto region, the wine could be drunk chilled in the summer. In common with all reds from Tuscany, the 1988 is superior to the 1989.
HDR; VIN

Grignolino d'Asti DOC, Renato Rabezzana 1988
B £c SS VE

A fresh, delicate and light red from the Grignolino grape, very much a regional variety. The wine won a commendation at the International Wine Challenge 1990. Renato Rabezzana's main wine, it is almost like a rosé, and provides a good alternative to white wine.
ORG

La Masseria, Vino da Tavola Rosso, G. Greco
B £b D ?

A Sicilian wine having a light red colour with a bouquet of cloves and well rounded fruity flavour. 13 per cent alcohol.
OWC

Nebbiolo d'Alba DOC, Renato Rabezzana 1987
C £c SS VE

From the same area and same grapes as Barolo, but without oak ageing and so with a less powerful overall character. Rather like a

Barolo for early drinking, a young full-bodied wine. Good deep structure.

ORG

Rubino di Poggio Antico, Poggio Antico 1987
B £b AIAB/D VE

Light, spicy wine on the palate, medium-bodied for easy drinking. From the same grapes as Chianti, the area from which it comes. The religously inspired co-operative who make the wine are not very keen on producing alcohol, preferring to make grape juice or table grapes. The wine lacks a certain imagination as a result, but it is nonetheless well made.

ORG

Rosso No.3, F. Croissant, 1989
B £c BIO ?

A light and fresh red, to drink on its own or with light food. Could be chilled in hot temperatures. Not very alcoholic, another of the Italian straightforward everyday wines.

SED

Rosso No.4, F. Croissant, 1989
C £c BIO ?

A blend of Tuscan grape varieties based on Sangiovese, the Chianti mainstay. Full fruity flavour and medium body, a wine typical of the area. Like one or two others in the region, not winning a high score for originality when it comes to naming the wine!

SED

Rosso, F. Croissant 1987
B £c BIO ?

A classier wine than the numbered ones above, made from late-harvested (and thus concentrated) Sangiovese grapes. This has a ruby red colour and good bouquet, with weight and character beyond its humble 'Vino da Tavola' description.

SED

Valpolicella Classico Superiore, Guerrieri-Rizzardi 1987/88
B £b/c IND No

Italian wines are so varied in quality and style that the well-known names need to be scrutinized in some detail. Guerrieri-Rizzardi is a top producer and this Valpolicella is a Classico Superiore, meaning

that it is from well-sited vineyards and a better quality wine. Medium-bodied and fruity, ready to drink now.
    VRT; HFW; COW

Amarone Valpolicella DOC Classico, Guerrieri-Rizzardi 1986
B £d/e IND VE
Another special from Italy. This is made from late-picked semi-dried grapes with concentrated sugar, producing a powerful and rich dry wine. Aged for at least two years in oak. The colour is red to brown and the overall style is full and weighty.
    VRT; HFW

SPAIN

Biovin Valdepenas DO 1988, Dionisio de Nova Morales
B £a VS VE
A delightful little wine, with warm, soft fruit. Medium-bodied, from the town of Valdepenas in La Mancha, south of Madrid, and one of the very few verified organic wines from Spain. Where are the rest? This wine is made from the Cencibel grape, otherwise known as Tempranillo. It produces a very friendly and fruity red. Unfortunately the 1989 wine was not released due to the inadequate quality of the vintage.
    HDR; VIN; VRT; SED

ENGLAND

Sedlescombe Vineyard Blackcurrant Wine
7 £b SA VE
We have classified this plum-coloured red wine by the white wine sweetness code rather than the red wine dryness code because it is medium-sweet. Most red wines are dry. This has a nicely balanced fruity flavour and strong blackcurrant bouquet. 8 per cent alcohol.
    SED

Sedlescombe Vineyard 1989 Red
A £d SA VE
A fresh, light to medium-bodied wine, dry, with a slight flavour of vanilla and blackcurrants. There are not many red wines made in England, and this is an interesting example of what can be achieved. At present only tiny quantities are produced. Roy Cook is currently

buying in the grapes but should have his own vines producing fruit soon. This is still at an experimental stage, including the propagation of an as yet unnamed variety and he is looking at the possibilities of using the Amurensis, a red variety whose original parentage lies far away on the Russian-Chinese border.

SED

AUSTRALIA

St Gilbert, Botobolar Vineyard 1987/8

▪▶ E £c NASAA V

One of the organic wines to have achieved consistently good press coverage over several vintages. Produced from the classic Australian blend of Shiraz and Cabernet Sauvignon, oak-aged for at least 2 years in small oak casks, this is a huge and powerful wine. A really gutsy mouthful, but still smooth and rich, with an excellent long finish. If you like big beefy wines, this is for you. Bronze Medal at the International Wine Challenge 1990.

VRT; SED; WRK

NEW ZEALAND

Waiheki Island, Stoneyridge 1988

▪▶ C £e IND ?

A youthful purple colour with the pungent bouquet of the fruit of the grapes, and finely balanced generous ripe flavour in the mouth. Smooth and weighty. Fine wine made from predominatly Cabernet Sauvignon with small amounts of Cabernet Franc and Merlot.

HFW

USA

Zinfandel, Frey Vineyards 1989

▪▶ D £c CCOF V

Still quite young and with good tannin, another chewy mouthful from the Frey brothers. Rich dark fruit flavours interwoven with the benefit of the oak in which it has matured. Spicy, peppery wine, well crafted and with masses of fruit.

VRT; SED; HDR; VIN

Cabernet Sauvignon, Frey Vineyards 1985
➤ D £d CCOF V

Another top quality 'new world' organic wine, available in relatively small quantities. The bouquet is strongly Cabernet, and the rich velvet and silk flavour make this smooth, powerful wine highly recommended. Excellent length in the mouth. Commendation at the International Wine Challenge 1990.
  VRT; SED

GERMANY

Armsheimer Goldstuckchen Haroldrebe, Kabinett Trocken 1986
A £a BOW VE

From the little-known Haroldrebe grape, a crossing from the Portugeiser and Limberger, and not one of the world's most highly-regarded varieties. It has the dubious attribute of being a pretty high yielder, up around the 140 hectolitre mark on many occasions. But this example is intriguing, with an unusual aroma and light, as you might expect.
  ROD

HUNGARY

Kekfrankos, Szekszardi MG Kombinat 1989
B £b EKO VE

Before researching this book, we thought, apparently in common with many others, that the Kekfrankos grape was a pretty close relation to the Gamay, grown mainly in Beaujolais and producer of lively, jammy, fruity reds usually best drunk young. This wine fits that description almost to the letter, and it even smells like Beaujolais. But we stand corrected; according to Jancis Robinson's mighty tome, *Vines, Grapes and Wines,* the Kekfrankos is related not to the Gamay but to the less resonant Blaufrankisch of eastern Europe. Nevertheless, this wine has a marvellous cherry-like colour and ripe juicy flavour. As with the two other Hungarian wines in this book it represents excellent value.
  VRT; HDR; VIN

Zweigelt, Szekszardi MG Kombinat 1989
C £b EKO VE

The Zweigelt grape is the result of a crossing of two different grapes and is named after its originator, Dr Zweigelt. Here it produces a firm medium to full-bodied wine with young fruit flavours. What stands out most is its tremendously fresh ripeness, as with the Kekfrankos, producing a wonderfully juicy mouthful. The rich fruit flavour gives an almost sweet background to what is an otherwise dry wine.

VRT; HDR; VIN; OWC

ROSÉ, CHAMPAGNE AND OTHER WINES

ROSÉ WINES

FRANCE

Domaine de Farlet Rosé, Vin de Pays des Collines de la Moure 1988
2 £a NP VE

Cherry-red, bright colour, bright flavour. From Cabernet Sauvignon and Cinsault grapes grown near Sète in the south of France. Soft and not too dry. Good value.
HDR; VIN

Château Canet, Bordeaux Rosé, 1989
2 £b IND V

Nice clear pink colour, mellow and fruity. Dry but not sharp, with a lovely ripe bouquet.
HDR; VIN

Château de Caraguilhes, Gris de Gris, Corbières, 1989
3 £b UNIA V

'Gris de Gris' is a term for a type of rosé wine. This is a very good estate and the rosé has excellent depth of colour, a spicy taste, and a fresh, clean finish. From Carignan, Grenache, Cinsault and Syrah grapes.
HFW; COW

Château St Jean d'Aumières, Coteaux de Languedoc 1989
3 £b IND V

Striking clean orange/pink colour, with a delicate strawberry nose. A smooth and full flavoured mouthful.
HFW; COW

Château de Prade Bordeaux Rosé, 1986
2 £b BIOPLAMPAC V
Predominantly Merlot grapes, mellow and soft.
  HDR; VIN

Château la Tour de l'Evêque, Côtes de Provence Petale de Rosé 1988
1 £b IND ?
Grenache and Cinsault. From hand-picked grapes, lightly pressed, made using cold fermentation techniques. Nice floral bouquet and light pink colour.
  HFW

Château Vieux-Gabiran, Bordeaux Rosé, 1989
1 £b NP VE
A light, fruity wine with strawberry overtones, delicate and with a lively colour.
  VRT

Michel Delacroix, Vin de Pays du Gard
1 £b NP ?
Deep pink colour, with a strong fruity bouquet, fresh and dry.
  OWC

Domaine St Apollinaire, Côtes du Rhône, Rosé 1989
1 £b DYN ?
From the very individualistic Domaine of M Daumas, a full flavoured rosé with good spicy bouquet and nice off-pink colour.
  VRT

Domaine St Cyriaque, Coteaux Varios VDQS, 1989
2 £b NP VE
A blend of southern varieties, the wine is pale in colour and straightforward in style.
  GJF

Domaine du Jas d'Esclans, Côtes de Provence, 1989
1 £b IND V
For drinking young and fresh. The pink colour is extracted by macerating the red grapes for a short period before fermenting the juice on its own. Salmon pink, straight as a whistle, with pleasantly restrained fruit character.
  HFW; VIN; HDR

Domaine de Dreuille, Cabernet d'Anjou, 1989
4 £b EAP VE

From the Cabernet Franc grape, a bit darker than previous years from this producer, with a delicate raspberry nose rather like the reds from the same grape in the Loire. Easy to drink.
VRT; SED

Domaine de Dreuille, Rosé de Loire, 1989
1/2 £b EAP VE

Rosé d'Anjou is medium dry, Rosé de Loire is dry. This has a deep pink colour and some 'bite' in the mouth, making it more akin to a crisp white wine. A good example.
VRT; SED

Gérard Leroux, Anjou Rosé, Demi-Sec
3 £b NP V

A pleasant medium dry rosé, with a clear salmon pink colour. An easy, fruity wine. Made from the unromantic-sounding Grolleau grape (sometimes spelt Groslot) which does not have the highest of reputations in the vine varieties status stakes. This is a much better wine than the grape variety would suggest. Gérard Leroux keeps his intervention into the natural processes to a minimum, and we commented favourably on the rustic style of his red. In his enthusiasm to produce a natural, full-flavoured product, filtration is kept to a minimum. In one vintage this was just too minimal and during the heat of the summer the natural yeasts remaining in the wine started to referment the sugars. Hey presto, instant sparkling wine as retailers around the UK found they had exploding bottles of rosé on their shelves. Lesson learned!
HDR; HFW; VIN; WHI

Gérard Leroux, Rosé de la Loire
1 £b NP V

Pretty dry this one, needs to go with food, but ideal if you like the almost parched twang of a crisp, crunchy wine. Serve chilled.
WHI

Listel Gris de Gris, Vin de Pays des Sables du Golfe du Lion
2 £b IND VE

'Gris de Gris' literally means 'grey from grey', which is actually rosé made from bluish-grey coloured grapes (as opposed to the purple to black of other regions). Follow that! Clean, fruity, eminently

quaffable and with plenty of light cherry-like flavour. From the giant Listel Company.
ABT

Mas de Gourgonnier, Coteaux d'Aix-en-Provence les Baux, 1989
2 £b NP ?
Excellent dry rosé made from the first run juice of the grapes. When the juice runs out it is naturally coloured by the grape skins and has a clear pink hue and big, rounded flavour. Good character.
OWC

Quotidianus, Vin de Table
1 £b NP ?
Not many times in this survey have we had to give a firm thumbs down to a wine, but this is one of those occasions. We found it astringent and unbalanced, lacking in fruit, and poorly made.
OWC

Christian and Nicole Dauny, Sancerre Rosé 1989
3 £c FESA VE
Made from Pinot Noir grapes grown at the eastern end of the Loire. A light to medium-bodied wine, too subdued in character to make a real impression. Dry, pleasant, light fruit flavours make it easy and delicate but not quite forceful enough. Nice acidity.
GJF

D'Heilly-Huberdeau, Bourgogne Rosé, 1987
1 £c FESA VE
Full coloured for a rosé, towards a light red; Pinot Noir grapes. Dry and fruity.
WHI

Château Barbeyrolles, Côtes de Provence, Petale de Rosé 1989
1 £d IND ?
Delicate pink colour, as the name suggests. Clean, dry, and fresh. Predominantly Cinsault with some Grenache.
HFW

ITALY

Pinot Rosé del Veneto, Zanette
2 £b AIAB/BIODYN VE
Soft, light, refreshing wine from Pinot Noir grapes. Only 10 per cent alcohol.
ORG

Rosa, F. Croissant, 1989
2 £b BIODYN ?
From the Tuscan Chianti grapes, Sangiovese and Canaiolo, crisp, fresh and young. One to serve chilled.
SED

Rosato 'Il Palagio' 1988
2 £b AIAB VE
Lively, fresh, perfumed and nicely fruity.
ORG

Rosolaccio Villa Angiolina
2 £b SES VE
Probably the driest of the Italian rosés, this has good bite and crisp acidity. Strong in alcohol at 13 per cent, vinified mostly as white wine and subsequently pale pink in colour. From Sangiovese grapes.
ORG

CHAMPAGNE

Note: All are non-vintage unless otherwise specified.

José Ardinat Carte d'Or, Brut
1 £e NP VE
Made solely from Pinot Noir and Pinot Meunier grapes — without any Chardonnay — this is excellent stuff. Lovely biscuity flavour, good strong and long-lasting fizz, the absence of Chardonnay gives the wine a full, robust character.
HDR; VIN; OWC

José Ardinat Carte d'Or, Demi Sec
6 £e NP VE
Exactly as for the Brut but with more natural sugar, making the wine suitable for serving with desserts.
HDR; VIN

José Ardinat Carte d'Or, Brut Cuvée Spéciale
1 £e NP VE

Picked out for special mention at the 1989 National Organic Wine Fair by *Wine Magazine* Publishing Editor Robert Joseph, who described it as 'Richly nutty and mature tasting, and would suit anyone who (like me) enjoys quite old-fashioned fizz'. Made from the best juice of several different years, the wine has a lovely toasty flavour and rich golden colour. From the same grapes as José Ardinat's other dry wine, Pinot Noir and Pinot Meunier.
EDB; HDR; VIN

André et Jacques Beaufort Grand Cru, Brut
1 £e GA VE

50 per cent Chardonnay, 50 per cent Pinot Noir, a fairly light and fresh Champagne. Elegant, subtle sparkle and nice length make this very good as an aperitif. Quite classical in style, mellow and biscuity.
HFW; COW; WHI

André et Jacques Beaufort Grand Cru, Demi-Sec
6 £e GA ?

Also 50 per cent Chardonnay, 50 per cent Pinot Noir, but not as dry as the Brut, with a higher residual sugar content. Equally delicious, with the same creamy character.
HFW; COW

André et Jacques Beaufort Grand Cru, Brut, 1979
1 £f GA VE

Differing from the normal Brut in being from the 1979 vintage specifically, it has plenty of body and a rounded fullness of flavour. Slightly more individual in style, it has the 'yeasty' smell which is characteristic of good Chardonnay.
HFW; COW; WHI

André et Jacques Beaufort Grand Cru, Brut Rosé
1 £f GA ?

Made from the same blend of Chardonnay and Pinot Noir as the Beauforts' white. It has a cheerful pink colour with good strong bubbles and rich fruit flavours.
HFW

Jean Bliard, 'Blanc de Blancs' Brut
1 £e UNIA VE

Made exclusively from the white Chardonnay grape which gives Champagne elegance and lightness. This has a fine, crisp flavour and light, fresh bouquet.
OWC; HDR; VIN

Jean Bliard, Brut Rosé
1 £e UNIA VE
With a faint pink colour and richly dry flavour, the wine has a light fruity bouquet. A succulent, lingering mouthful. Made by leaving the juice in contact with the red grape skins for just a short time, the result is an almost onion-pink colour. From Pinot Meunier and Pinot Noir grapes, with low SO_2 like all M Bliard's wines.
HDR; VIN; OWC

Jean Bliard, 'Cuvée des Trois Cépages', Brut
1 £e UNIA VE
As the name Cuvée des Trois Cépages indicates, this is made from a blend of the three famous Champagne grapes, Chardonnay, Pinot Noir and Pinot Meunier. Clear straw colour, light floral bouquet, fairly weighty and slightly bitter flavour. Based in Hautvillers, north of Epernay in the Vallée de la Marne, the cellars are within a stone's throw of the church where Dom Perignon, the legendary creator of Champagne, was buried. The Bliards have 4 hectares of vines, enabling them to sell a total of approximately 15–20,000 bottles per year, which is not a lot by conventional commercial standards. All their Champagnes are made without fining, the wines simply being left to settle and clear naturally over the winter.
HDR; VIN; VRT; OWC

Jean Bliard, 'Cuvée de la Marne', Brut
1 £e UNIA VE
This is the second string wine from Jean Bliard's 'Cuvée des Trois Cépages', made from the second pressing of the grapes. It lacks the finesse or character of the first wine, being coarser in its overall style. Nevertheless it retains a rich golden colour with good 'mousse' (bubbles), and will be very acceptable fizz for everyday.
OWC

Jean Bliard, 'Doré Trois Cépages', Demi-sec
6 £e UNIA VE
As for the Cuvée des Trois Cépages Brut, but with the extra added natural grape sugar making it a sweeter wine.
HDR; VIN

Serge Faust, Carte d'Or Brut
1 £e UNIA VE

Serge Faust is José Ardinat's father-in-law. They work together to produce these delightful Champagnes, dividing the spoils between them, using their own labels to share the joint effort. Otherwise the Ardinat and Faust wines are absolutely identical. This one is the same as José Ardinat's Carte d'Or.
    SED; VRT

Serge Faust Cuvée de Réserve
1 £e UNIA VE

For this one — excellent — see the description for Ardinat's Cuvée Spéciale.
    VRT

Poirrier Cuvée Spéciale Brut Extra-Dry, 1985
1 £f NP VE

From a blend of grapes including the Petit Meslier, a rarity these days. The Meslier produces wines of high acidity and this adds bite to the overall flavour. Creamy-textured, buttery taste with crisp acidity.
    VRT

Yves Ruffin, Cuvée G. de Goujon, Extra Brut
1 £f UNIA V

Extra Brut means super dry. This is clean as a whistle, lovely pale yellow, as dry as you are likely to find, but definitely not acidic. The wine is well made, with both fruity elegance and nice yeasty nose. From a Premier Cru vineyard, second only to Grand Cru in quality designation, it is a blend of 60 per cent Pinot Noir and 40 per cent Chardonnay. Aged for two years prior to release, the wine is a limited edition with only 2,800 bottles available in 1990.
    GJF

SPARKLING WINES

FRANCE

All are made using the champagne method unless otherwise stated.

Anjou Brut, Domaine de Dreuillé
2 £d EAP VE

The best of Yves Freulon's Chardonnay and Chenin Blanc grapes go to make this delicious sparkling wine. From the lower Loire, it has a delicate aroma of honey with a powerful dry flavour.
VRT

Bacchus Brut, Bordeaux, Deffarge—Garcia 1987/8
1 £c FESA ?

From the Semillon grape, with decent weight in the mouth, full but sufficiently crisp to balance well. Pale golden colour. Don't be misled into thinking that the reference to Bacchus in the name refers to the grape type: it is presumably a comment on the revelry the wine elicits!
OWC

Bacchus, Bordeaux Rosé 1987
1 £c FESA V

Another rosé to evoke the taste and smell of strawberries. Good length, nicely dry. 100 per cent Cabernet Franc grapes.
OWC

Le Bourdieu, Bordeaux
1 £d FNAB V

Semillon and Ugni Blanc grapes, pale coloured wine with good fizz, nice balance and plenty of fruit in the bouquet.
HFW; WHI

Le Bourdieu, Bordeaux Rosé
1 £d FNAB V

Cabernet Sauvignon and Merlot grapes. This is an aromatic wine with an inviting bouquet, quite full and fruity flavour.
HFW; WHI

Bossard-Thuaud, Guy Bossard
3 £c/d FESA VE

A very crisp dry white following the style of his excellent still wines. Made from Muscadet grapes with a little Gros Plant.
SED; VRT; WHI; OWC

Blanc de Blancs 'St Geneviève', Bourgogne, Alain Guillot
2 £d FNAB VE

Chardonnay grapes, a dry sparkler to drink fresh and young. Like all Alain Guillot's wines, no SO$_2$, as natural a wine as possible.
   WHI

Blanquette de Limoux, Bernard Delmas
2 £c UNIA No
Terrific sparkling wine from the Mauzac grape. Blanquette de Limoux is not particularly well-known in the UK, but when well made, as here, it rivals the more expensive sparkling wines. Lovely green colour and bright nutty flavour, strong and full of character. Good long-lasting fizz.
   HDR; VIN; WRK; THR

Blanquette de Limoux, Cuvée Malvina, G. Buoro
2 £c NP V
From Gino Buoro's 50-hectare estate where he produces Blanquette, dry whites, and fruity reds. Into his fifth year as an organic grower, this is a blend of Mauzac with a little Chardonnay and Chenin Blanc. The wine, from near the southern town of Limoux, has a strong nutty flavour typical of the Mauzac grape.
   SED; VRT

Clairette de Die, Brut, Achard Vincent
1 £c NP VE
A terrific Méthode Champenoise wine from the Clairette grape. 'Die' is not a curse but a beautiful little town in the Drôme valley, itself east of the Rhône. A mountainous region producing some unique wines. This one is refreshingly dry with a superb long-lasting sparkle and lovely yellow colour. Silver Medal, Paris 1990.
   COW; HDR; HFW; SED; VIN; OWC

Clairette de Die, Tradition, Achard Vincent
6 £c/d NP VE
This differs from the Méthode Champenoise Demi-Sec because it is made using the Methode Dioise, an alternative regional method of producing natural sparkle. The wine is fermented at a very low temperature for a long period before being filtered once it has reached about 6 degrees alcohol. It is then bottled and secondary fermentation increases the alcohol and creates the fizz. This produces a wine of only about 8.5 per cent alcohol, crammed with the natural sweetness of the unfermented sugars. From Muscat and Clairette grapes it is wonderfully juicy and grapey, with a strong

yellow colour. Best drunk within two years of bottling while the freshness and life remain. Commended at the International Wine Challenge 1990.

COW; HDR; HFW; VIN; OWC

Côtes du Jura Brut, Michel Terrier
2 £c FESA V

Dry, fresh white fizz from France's eastern outpost. A wine to keep your friends guessing — how many have heard of, let alone tasted a wine from this region, especially a sparkling wine?

WHI

Crémant d'Alsace, Eugène Meyer 1986
2 £d D VE

From the Pinot Blanc (or Klevner as the Pinots are known locally) grape, a champagne method treat. Crémant literally means 'creaming', and this wine has a suitable cream-like background. Crémant wines have slightly less pressure in the bottle than Champagne, and hence are a bit more relaxed.

HFW

Crémant de Bourgogne Blanc de Blancs, Brut, Alain Verdet
2 £d FNAB V

Chardonnay and Aligoté grapes, fairly dry with an almost lemony appeal. Nice fizz.

OWC

Cuvée de la Boissière, Brut, J. Brard Blanchard
1 £c NP ?

Bone-dry, clean, light and crisp. Unusual wine from this region, best known for its cognac. Recommended as an aperitif or base for mixing with a fruit liqueur.

OWC

Fleur de Muscat, Foxonet
7 £c NP VE

An intensely flavoured sparkling wine from the Muscat grape, rich and medium-sweet. It has a powerful aroma from the grapey character of the Muscat, and a full-bodied fruity flavour. Not Méthode Champenoise.

VRT

Les Fournaches, Bourgogne Rosé, Alain Verdet
2 £d FNAB VE
Pinot Noir grapes again, good dry, rounded pink sparkler.
  WHI

Saumur Brut, Gérard Leroux 1987
1 £c/d NP V
From the Chenin Blanc grapes, Saumur is well known for its champagne method sparkling wines. This example has a forthright, biscuity flavour and good firm colour. At half the price of Champagne it's good value.
  HDR; VIN; VRT; WHI

Saumur, Gérard Leroux, Demi-Sec
6 £c NP V
As for the Brut but with the 'dosage' of naturally sweet juice added at the end of the winemaking process to produce a medium dry wine.
  HFW; COW; WHI

Saumur Rosé Méthode Champenoise, Gérard Leroux
1 £c NP V
A fine pink sparkler, bold pink in colour, clean and surprisingly dry. Grolleau grapes.
  HDR; VIN

Vin Mousseux, Clos St Martin, Doux
6 £c NP ?
This is carbonated white wine made from Muscat grapes grown in the Languedoc region. Quite fresh and appealing, but without the class of other wines made using the champagne method.
  HFW

GERMANY

Scheurebe Extra Trocken Sekt 1987, H Thiel
1 £d BOW VE
An extra dry wine from the Scheurebe grape, now regaining popularity in this country for its still wines. Scheurebe has the potential to make truly delightful wines and this champagne method version (the method for all the Sekt) combines nice fruit and fine dryness, retaining richness of flavour.
  ROD

⚑ *Morio-Muskat Halbtrocken Sekt, 1988, H. Thiel*
🍾 2 £e BOW VE

Medium dry rich flavoured sparkling wine from the Morio-Muskat grape, good fruity bouquet. This is the sweetest of the four sparkling wines available from Haus Thiel.

ROD

⚑ *Spätburgunder-Rotsekt Trocken, 1987, H. Thiel*
🍾 A £e BOW VE

Spätburgunder is another name for the famous Pinot Noir grape, doyen of Burgundy and main contender to rival the great wines of the Medoc in boardrooms around the world. In Germany the grape often struggles to make red wine at all, the climate leading to a pale imitation of the noble French juice. The flavour here is fairly restrained and mild, while producing some fruit and character. Interesting stuff.

ROD

⚑ *Spätburgunder Weissherbst Extra Trocken Sekt 1988, H. Thiel*
🍾 1 £e BOW VE

A pink sparkling Méthode Champenoise, extra dry, nice delicate colour and fragrance.

ROD

ITALY

⚑ *Rosé, F. Croissant, 1988*
🍾 1 £d BIO VE

Extra dry pink sparkler from the Italian/German partnership of Gabi and Fritz Croissant in Tuscany. Fine bouquet and well-integrated flavours.

SED

⚑ *Rosso di Vignano, F. Croissant 1987*
🍾 1 £e BIO ?

The favourite of the producers, a delicious, strong and robustly flavoured red sparkling wine from Sangiovese grapes.

SED

SPAIN

⚑ *Cava Sparkling Extra Brut, Albet i Noya*
🍾 1 £c VS VE

An extra dry wine, from the Penedes region near Barcelona. The popularity of the non-organic Cava (Méthode Champenoise) wines in recent years testifies to their quality and value. This, the only organic Cava, is very traditional in style, having a nice yeasty bouquet and distinctive full-flavoured texture. Likely to make friends or enemies — sufficiently distinctive not to get a middle-of-the-road response.
HDR; VIN

ENGLAND

1989 Sedlescombe Quality Sparkling Wine, Brut
1 £e SA VE
Catch this one early as stocks are restricted each year. The wine is the UK's first organic sparkler, made in the traditional champagne method from a blend of Kerner and Seyval grapes. A vintage wine, 11 per cent alcohol.
SED

FORTIFIED WINES

Crème de Framboise (Raspberry) 18 per cent, A Verdet
9 £e FNAB V
Alain Verdet's wines from the Hautes Côtes de Nuits in Burgundy are amongst the best organic wines on the market, and his standards are maintained with his range of 'Crèmes'. These are fruit liqueurs made by macerating the pure fruit in alcohol and sugar. The concentration of the bouquet and flavour is almost overwhelming; it is rather like tasting a natural essence of the fruits! The liqueurs are usually added to dry white or sparkling wines to make a flavoured drink for special occasions.
VRT; HFW; COW; WHI; OWC

Crème de Mûre (Blackberries) 20 per cent, A Verdet
9 £d/e FNAB V
HFW; COW; WHI; OWC

Crème de Pêche (Peach) 18 per cent, A Verdet
9 £e FNAB V
VRT; HFW; WHI; OWC

Crème de Cassis (blackcurrant) de Bourgogne, 20 per cent,
A Verdet
   9 £d/e FNAB V
VRT; HFW; COW; WHI; OWC

Fruit Liqueurs, Maison L'Héraud — Orange, Almond, Apricot,
Blackcurrant, Raspberry and Pear
   8 £f IND VE
At the same luxurious level of quality as Alain Verdet's liqueurs
come those from Maison L'Héraud. Whereas Alain's are fruit
macerated in alcohol and sugar, these are fruit macerated in organic
cognac. Presented in lovely frosted glasses, the contents are every
bit as good as the presentation. They range in alcohol content from
22 per cent for the Raspberry to 35 per cent for the Orange. Our
favourite is a toss up between the Pear and Raspberry; the most
unusual is the subtly flavoured Almond. The fruit flavours are just
slightly less straightforward than Alain's liqueurs, the cognac giving
a mellow background tinge to the fruit. The quality is outstanding.
   HDR; VIN

Syrop de Myrtille, Claude Pascolo
   7 £d FNAB V
Bilberry liqueur to add to the organic cocktails or spice up the ice
cream.
   WHI

Vinoix, François Clot
   7 £e NP V
Full of natural sugars, but with a sherry-like consistency, this is a
brown coloured drink made from an organic Côtes du Rhône wine
base and organically grown walnuts. Unusual, and well worth
experimenting with.
   WHI

Macvin, Terrier
   7 £d NP V
17 per cent alcohol, very rich in natural sugar, to drink either as an
aperitif or a dessert wine. The process involves stopping
fermentation early, fortifying with eau-de-vie and then ageing for
2–3 years in oak. Smooth and silky.
   WHI

Muscat de Rivesaltes, Coronat
9 £c NP VE

Muscat de Rivesaltes is a luscious sweet wine from the Roussillon region of southern France. It is made from varieties of the Muscat grape, and is produced by adding neutral alcohol to the partially fermented wine, and at the same time stopping the fermentation before all the sugars have been fermented out, so leaving the wine naturally sweet. The character of Muscat is very grapey, with good concentrated flavour. The freshness of the bouquet and flavour is at its best when the wine is young. As it ages, the colour darkens and the flavour becomes deeper but less aromatic. Drink this one as a dessert wine or chilled as an aperitif.

VRT

Vieux Rivesaltes, Coronat 1980
8 £c NP V

A medium sweet fortified red wine rather like a tawny Port. Made from the Grenache Noir grape, the wine has turned golden brown as it has matured. Full-bodied and rich but not cloying.

VRT

Domaine Aimé Fontanel Muscat de Rivesaltes 1987
7 £c IND ?

100 per cent Muscat grapes, produced from a very low yield giving less than one bottle per vine. Pale gold in colour, an exotic flowery bouquet followed by a richly sweet mouthful of flavours. You could serve it chilled as an aperitif or at room temperature as a dessert.

HFW; COW

OTHER ORGANIC DRINKS

Cognac ★★★ Brard Blanchard
N/A £e/f NP VE

Jacques and Dany Blanchard make their fine brandies from Ugni Blanc grapes, all hand-picked. The hallmark of good brandies such as these is their smooth, rounded flavour and silky, mellow character. The three star, aged for at least 2½ years, is warm and subtle.

HFW; OWC

Cognac, VSOP Brard Blanchard
N/A £f NP VE

The next quality stage up from the three star, this is aged for 7 years and has a little extra all round — more concentrated flavour, lovely long lingering aroma. Smooth and without a hint of harshness.

HFW; COW; WHI; OWC

Maison L'Héraud Cognacs
N/A £f IND VE

The range of cognacs from the estate of Maison L'Héraud are right at the top end of the quality bracket — and this is reflected in the price! Starting with the three star at one end of the spectrum, the most expensive, the 50-year old 'Paradis', costs a staggering £215 a bottle. The older the cognac, the smoother and more expensive it gets. Beautifully packaged, these cognacs are made without the addition of water to dilute them. First class.

- Cognac Spéciale Trois Etoiles 3 Years Old 40 per cent, Maison L'Héraud
- Cognac VSOP 5 Years Old 40 per cent, Maison L'Héraud
- Réserve du Templier 10 Years Old 42 per cent, Maison L'Héraud

- Vieille Réserve 20 Years Old 43 per cent, Maison L'Héraud
- X.O. 30 Years Old 44 per cent, Maison L'Héraud
- Paradis 50 Years Old 52 per cent, Maison L'Héraud

HDR; VIN

Cognac VSOP, Guy Pinard
N/A £f NP VE

A single vineyard cognac, smooth and mellow, matured in oak. Friendly and mild.
VRT; OWC

Cognac Napoléon, Guy Pinard
N/A £e/f NP VE

From the top of his range, pale gold colour and with extra smoothness.
VRT; OWC

Pineau des Charentes, Maison L'Héraud
6 £d IND VE

This producer makes both white and rosé Pineau at 17 per cent alcohol. Unfermented organic grape juice is blended with cognac to make a delicious fresh fruit drink with a ripe bouquet.
HDR

Pineau de Charentes Blanc, Brard Blanchard
8 £c NP ?

An overriding flavour of the fruit of the grapes gives a nice balance to the power of the cognac. Aged in oak barrels for three years. Winner of a commendation at the International Wine Challenge 1990.
HFW; OWC; VRT

Pineau de Charentes Rosé, Brard Blanchard
8 £d NP ?

This rosé has a strawberryish flavour which blends nicely with the natural sweetness of the juice. Good with dessert and rich, exotic foods.
HFW; OWC

Très Vieil Armagnac, J. Michaud 1962, 1969, 1974
N/A £f NP ?

These three vintages of M Michaud's Armagnac are all aged for at least 13 years in local Armagnac oak barrels. Armagnac is coming out of the shadow of cognac a bit these days, and examples such as these will help enormously. Produced in the Gascony region south west of Bordeaux, now much better known in the UK for the ubiquitous dry white wine Vin de Pays de Gascogne, Armagnac shares with cognac the use of the Ugni Blanc grape. As the Armagnac ages, so it becomes smoother, rounder and softer. The power of the alcohol remains but much of the harshness subsides.

HFW; COW(74)

Eau de Vie de Poire William, Verdet
8 £f FNAB V

45 per cent alcohol, a strong and aromatic spirit made from pears. Recommended as a digestif.

WHI

Grappa di Chianti, F. Croissant, 1987
1 £e BIO VE

The mighty Grappa, organic firewater for the brave. The Italian answer to Schnapps, a clear spirit distilled from the grape skins of the 1987 Chianti vintage.

SED

BEER AND LAGER

Golden Promise Organic Beer
N/A SA VE

The first commercially brewed beer, as distinct from lager, comes from the excellent Caledonian brewery in Edinburgh. Their old 'coppers' date back to 1869 and are still used today to process the organic malt and hops. The beer is strong at 5 per cent alcohol and comes in 50cl bottles. It has a pronounced rich malty flavour and is somewhere between a Pale and Brown ale.

HDR; VIN; OWC

Lincoln Green Lager
N/A SA VE

This UK-brewed beer hit the shelves in 1990 and is becoming fairly widely available. With a lower original gravity than the Pinkus from Germany (see below), it has greater taste similarity to conventional lager. Packed in 440 ml cans, it is excellent value for an organic product. 4.5 per cent alcohol, imported German hops.

VRT; WHI

Pinkus Special Organic Lager
N/A BIO VE

The Müller family have been making specialist beers at their brewery in Münster for 200 years. This organic lager is made solely from water, yeast, and organic hops and barley. It also conforms to the German purity laws, the Reinheitsgebot, which does not specify that the ingredients must be organically grown but prohibits additives. The Pinkus Special Organic Lager is bottled in both 33cl and 50cl bottles. Top fermented and stored for 3 months prior to bottling, it has a marvellously golden colour and a crisp, dry, light flavour with a bitter background. The contrast with sweetened commercial lagers is huge. Unfiltered, it is not star-bright but has a dull sheen. Filtration (which is carried out for the US market) removes a little of the flavour as well as the light sediment.

ORG; HDR; VIN

Ross Brewery Beers
N/A IND No

Mike Ross has produced two interesting beers using mostly organic ingredients at his very small independent brewery in Bristol. His Hartcliffe Bitter is the more commercial beer, although the Clifton Dark has a good, strong malty flavour. Both are 1040-1045 O.G. (around 4 per cent alcohol) and bottled in pints. The beers are made from organic barley but the hops (a small part of the total ingredients) are not organic. Bottle conditioned, with no added carbon dioxide, there is a sediment. Store the beers cool and allow to settle for 24 hours before opening.

ORG

CIDER AND COUNTRY WINES

Avalon, Natural Dry Still Cider
1 SA VE

A very traditional cider from Shepton Mallet in Somerset, its dry refreshing appley bite really reflects a local style. More for drinking out of a wine glass than a pint beer mug, it is a real contrast to the sweetened commercial varieties. One of Hugh Tripp's traditional practices is to press the apples in an old hand-turned cider press to extract maximum colour and flavour. The cider is stored in old oak rum barrels to impart a mellow background flavour. 5 to 6 per cent alcohol, stronger than commercial cider.

HDR; VIN

Avalon, Natural Sparkling Cider
1 SA VE

Made in the same way as the still cider, but with a naturally created sparkle. The secondary fermentation in the bottle gives off carbon dioxide which makes the cider fizz. Best to let the sediment created by this fermentation settle out by leaving the cider for 48 hours before opening — preferably in the fridge. A touch less dry than his still cider.
HDR; VIN

Avalon, Cider Wine
1 SA VE

A unique product, made initially in the same way as the dry ciders, but fermented for longer and then stored prior to bottling, to allow it to develop. The result is an intriguing hybrid between wine and cider with a strong individual character. It has a warm, rounded, almost caramelly taste.
HDR; VIN

Dunkertons Court Royal Cider
3 SA VE

A still medium dry cider in litre bottles from the rare Court Royal cider apple, made in Herefordshire. This is the only single apple variety that Ivor and Susie Dunkerton make which currently has organic status. A pity, because it is delicious. Like the ciders from the Avalon property in Somerset, it has a character strongly based in the traditions of its region. This is added to by the Dunkertons' exemplary insistence on reintroducing and retaining classical cider apple varieties which have been fast fading out of existence. The cider has no added water and so is strong in alcohol — 8 per cent, which is the equivalent of some German wines, so drink with your liver in mind. Naturally cloudy.
DUN; HDR; VIN

Dunkertons Dry Organic Cider
1 SA VE

This blended cider comes from some of the many traditional cider apple varieties used by the Dunkertons. They have almost magical names — this one is made from Brown Snout, Foxwhelp, White Norman and Yarlington Mill. Naturally cloudy, it is drier than the Court Royal, with a generous full flavour and mellow character. 6.3 per cent alcohol.
DUN; HDR; VIN

Dunkertons Perry
3 SA VE

Perry is to pears what cider is to apples. Perry is not made by many people in the UK nowadays, and this is the only organic version that we know of. It has a lovely wild pear bouquet and firm, concentrated dry flavour. Made from trees, some now up to 300 years old, of the Merrylegs, Red Horse, Moorcroft, and Painted Lady varieties. 7 per cent alcohol.
DUN; HDR; VIN

Sedlescombe Apple Wine
2 SA VE

From a blend of Bramley and Newton's Wonder Apples, this aromatically fresh dry wine is light and refreshing with a crisp finish. 8 per cent alcohol.
SED

LOW ALCOHOL WINES

Pétillant de Raisin, Domaine de Matens, 3 per cent
7 NP VE

Pétillant de Raisin is a genuine low alcohol product, not a de-alcoholized wine (where the wine is made as normal and then processed to take out the alcohol). The grapes are partially fermented, so that the fermentation is stopped when the wine has only converted a little of the natural sugars into alcohol, leaving it naturally sweet and less than 3 per cent alcohol. As the carbon dioxide gas given off in the course of fermentation is trapped and kept in the bottle, the wine is naturally sparkling. Pétillant de Raisin (literally, sparkle from the grape), can be produced in various places but this one comes from Gaillac in south west France. It has an excellent fizz and rich creamy bouquet which was once rather negatively described as being similar to a freshly-opened can of paint! But we liked it.
HDR; VIN

Pétillant de Raisin, Cuvée Réserve, Domaine de Cantalauze
7 NP V

Just down the road from Domaine de Matens is Domaine de Cantaluze, the only other certified organic Pétillant de Raisin. Another delicious drink, we found it slightly less fresh and fruity than the Matens, with a less pronounced bouquet, but more direct in its appeal.
OWC

JUICES

Parents and others worried that many drinks contain additives and possibly pesticide residues need look no further for a safe alternative. Organic fruit or vegetable juices are the answer and they are becoming increasingly easy to find. Below is our selection of juices available at the present time.

Apple Juices

Domaine de Balazut
Fresh, clean apple flavour. FESA organic symbol.
  WHI

Bionova
Variable colour and flavour, contains sediment but very delicious. Biodynamically produced in Holland.
  HDR; VIN

Aspall
Has been produced in Suffolk for many years and has certainly stood the test of time. Soil Association symbol. Widely available.

Copella
Pressed on the farm near Colchester in Essex. Easy to drink. Organic Farmers and Growers Symbol as well as the Soil Association's.

Pear Juice

Domaine de Balazut
Light, fruity, essence of pears. FESA organic symbol.
  WHI

Grape Juices

White Grape Juice, Guy Bossard
Gros Plant and Muscadet young vines produce this juice which is the driest of all but still sweet. Probably the nearest in flavour to a wine if, like us, you can't abide de-alcoholized wines. No sulphur dioxide in the finished product. FESA organic symbol.
  HDR; VIN

Domaine de Balazut Grape Juice

Another of the fresh and fruity organic grape juices, tastes much more natural than the supermaket cartons. FESA organic symbol.
 WHI

Domaine Bourdieu Pur Jus de Raisin Blanc, 'Ambre'

We found this just a little cloying in its sweetness, not sufficiently clean, although pleasant enough. Probably better a bit watered down to temper the natural sugar. UNIA organic symbol.
 HFW

Coronat Pur Jus de Raisin Muscat Blanc

Hard to beat the Muscat grape when it comes to revelling in luscious grape flavours. Another juice that has so much natural flavour and sugar that it can almost be treated as concentrated and made to go further by adding water. Nature et Progrès organic symbol.
 HFW

Pierre Arnaud Red Grape Juice

Pierre Arnaud makes two different juices, one pure Muscat and the other a blend of regional grapes. The Muscat is a little juicier; the blend has a bit more weight to it. Both are pretty sweet and can be watered down a lot. When turned into wine these grapes form part of the Cave La Vigneronne Côtes Du Rhône organic wine. Good stuff, coming top in our children's poll of the juices on offer. Nature et Progrès organic symbol.
 HDR; VIN

Cherry Juice

Rabenhorst

Cherry nectar produced from Morello cherries in West Germany. Organic verifying body not stated on label but we were assured that the growers are members of the German ANOG organization.

Orange Juice

Voelkel

Very heavy sediment, extremely dry but fruity and thirst-quenching. Made by a Biodynamic co-operative in Barcelona. Carries the Demeter biodynamic symbol. Imported by Bio-Dynamic Supplies.

Mixed Fruit Juice

Bionova

Containing apples, pears, rosehips, blackberries, raspberries and plums, this heavily sedimented juice is too sweet for our taste but we're sure children would love it. Fruits are either organic, biodynamic or wild. Carries the Biodyn symbol. Made in Holland.
  HDR; VIN

Vegetable Juices

The organic vegetable juices we sampled all had very strong flavours and as well as tasting delicious chilled, make ideal bases for soups, etc.

Eden produce three organic vegetable juices — carrot, beetroot and celery, all of which carry the Demeter symbol.

Rabenhorst also produce three organic vegetable juices — carrot, beetroot and tomato, and whilst their label does not carry an organic symbol, we were told that the growers belong to the German ANOG organic organization.

Some supermarkets now sell organic juices but if you can't find them locally, it's best to search wholefood shops and delicatessens and ask the owners to get some in for you!

Suppliers for Juices

Aspalls, Aspall Hall, Debenham, Nr Stowmarket, Suffolk IP14 6PD. Tel. 0728 860510

Peakes Organic Foods, Hill Farm, Boxford, Suffolk CO6 5NY. Tel. 0787 210348

Haus Rabenhorst. Importer: John Powell Wines, Harding Way, St Ives, Cambridgeshire PE17 4WR. Tel. 0480 63590

Eden-Waren. Distributor: Leisure Drinks, Castle Donington, Derbyshire.

Voelkel. Importer: Biodynamic Supplies, Woodman Lane, Clent, Nr Stourbridge, West Midlands DY9 9PX. Tel. 0562 884933.

7

THE HIGH STREET

Most of the supermarket chains, specialist wine merchants and off-licence groups are now interested in stocking organic wines. Within many of these organizations there are buyers who see beyond the profit motive alone, and who have a desire to choose organic where possible — quality, price and commercial viability permitting. In this, Safeway have been market leaders, but we can be sure to see an increasing number of organic wines in a variety of other high street stores in the future.

Availability of wines in large chain stores is likely to fluctuate, as organic wines are, by nature, produced in limited quantities. The information in the next section was correct at the time of writing. Those companies not listed either did not stock any organic wines, or were unable to give us the information. The low alcohol Pétillant wines of Listel are not listed here, although sold in several chains with an organic ticket, because they do not meet our criteria for organic classification. (See note on Listel on pages 81–82.)

OFF-LICENCE AND WINE MERCHANT CHAINS

The address given is the head office.

Augustus Barnett Ltd

Augustus Barnett Ltd, 3 The Maltings, Wetmore Road, Burton-on-Trent, Staffordshire DE14 1SE. Tel. 0283 512550

White

Domaine de Villeroy-Castellas, Vin de Pays des Sables du Golfe du Lion 1988/9 (page 97)

Red

Domaine Bosquet-Canet, Cabernet Sauvignon, Vin de Pays des Sables du Golfe du Lion, 1988 (page 144)
Domaine des Soulié, St Chinian, 1989 (page 147)
Mas de la Dame, Coteaux d'Aix-en-Provence, Les Baux (page 153)

Rosé

Listel Gris de Gris, Vin de Pays des Sables du Golfe du Lion (page 169)

Blayneys (North of England, selected stores)

Blayneys, Riverside Road, Sunderland, Tyne and Wear SR5 3JW. Tel. 091 548 8866

White

Château le Barradis Bergerac Sauvignon Sec (page 104)

Red

Domaine de Farlet Merlot, Vin de Pays des Collines de la Moure 1988 (page 145)

Bottoms Up Wine Superstores

Bottoms Up Wine Superstores, Astra House, Edinburgh Way, Harlow, Essex CM20 2BE. Tel. 0279 451145

White

Château le Barradis Bergerac Sauvignon Sec (page 104)
Château Caderonne Limoux 1989 (page 96)
Rivaner, St Ursula 1989 (page 111)

Red

Albaric, Vin de Pays du Gard (page 140)
Côtes du Rhône, Pierre Perrin (page 155)
Château Vignelaure, Coteaux d'Aix-en-Provence, 1985 (page 151)

Majestic Wine Warehouses
(12-bottle case sales only)

Majestic Wine Warehouses, 421 New Kings Road, London SW6 4RN. Tel. 071 731 3131

Red

Domaine de L'Attilon Merlot, Vin de Pays des Bouches du Rhône, 1989 (page 156)

Oddbins

Oddbins, Dunsford Industrial Estate, 31-33 Weir Road, Wimbledon, London SW19 8UG. Tel. 081 879 1199

White

Riesling Kabinett Dienheimer Paterhof, Bruder Dr Becker, 1989, halbtrocken (page 110)

Red

Côtes du Rhône, Vignoble de la Jasse 1989 (page 156)
Château de Beaucastel, Châteauneuf-du-Pape, 1987 (page 157)
Mas de Daumas Gassac, Languedoc 1988 (page 148)

Threshers/Wine Rack

Threshers/Wine Rack, Sefton House, 42 Church Road, Welwyn Garden City, Herts AL8 6PJ. Tel. 0707 328244
　Threshers also own a chain of specialist wine shops trading under the name Wine Rack.

Available at Threshers and Wine Rack:
Sparkling
Blanquette de Limoux, Bernard Delmas (page 176)

Available in Wine Rack stores only:
White
Sylvaner, QbA, Dr Becker, Ludwigshöhe Teufelskopf, 1986 (page 111)
Domaine de la Parentière Muscadet de Sèvre et Maine sur Lie 1989/90 (page 99)

Red
St Gilbert—Botobolar Vineyard 1987/8 (page 164)

Wizard Wine Warehouses (South of England, 13 stores)
(12-bottle case sales only)

Wizard Wine Warehouses, 6 Theobold Court, Theobold Street, Borehamwood, Hertfordshire WD6 4RN. Tel. 081 207 4455

White
Château Large-Malartic Entre-Deux-Mers 1989 (page 92)

Red
Château Large-Malartic Bordeaux 1988 (page 127)

SUPERMARKETS

Asda

Asda Stores, Asda House, Southbank, Great Wilson Street, Leeds LS1 5AD. Tel. 0532 435435

White
Muscadet de Sèvre et Maine sur Lie, Guy Bossard 1989 (page 99)
Château Meric Graves Supérieur 1989 (page 92)

Red
Domaine de Bargac, Vin de Pays du Gard, 1989 (page 143)
Organic Claret, Château Vieux-Georget Bordeaux 1988 (page 127)

Co-op/Leos (selected stores)

Co-op/Leos, 29 Dantzic Street, Manchester M4 4BA. Tel. 061 832 8152

White
Château le Barradis Bergerac Sauvignon Sec (page 104)
Muscadet de Sèvre et Maine sur Lie, Domaine de la Parentière, 1989 (page 99)

Red
Domaine de Clairac Joubio, Vin de Pays de L'Hérault (page 144)
Côtes du Rhône, Vignoble de la Jasse, 1989 (page 156)

E H Booth and Co (20 stores in Lancs, Cumbria and Cheshire)

E H Booth and Co, 4-6 Fishergate, Preston, Lancs. Tel. 0772 51701

White
Domaine de Villeroy–Castellas Sauvignon Blanc, Vin de Pays des Sables du Golfe du Lion (page 97)
Blanc de Blancs, Guy Bossard (page 98)
Chardonnay, Millton Vineyard 1988/9 (page 124)

Red

Domaine Bosquet-Canet Cabernet Sauvignon 1988, Vin de Pays des Sables du Golfe du Lion (page 144)
Domaine du Jas D'Esclans, Côtes de Provence, 1986 (page 152)
Château de Prade Bordeaux Supérieur, 1986 (page 130)
Simone Couderc Coteaux du Languedoc 1987 (page 142)

Champagne

José Ardinat, Carte d'Or, Brut Cuvée Spéciale (page 172)

Safeway

Safeway plc, Argyll Stores Ltd, Argyll House, Millington Road, Hayes, Middlesex UB3 4AY. Tel. 081 848 8744

White

St Ursula Scheurebe 1989 (page 111)
Château Canet Entre-Deux-Mers 1989 (page 91)
Dienheimer Tafelstein Kabinett, Bruder Dr Becker, QmP (page 112)
Flonheimer Adelberg Kerner Spätlese, Gebruder Werner 1988 (page 113)

Red

Safeway Organic Vin de Table (page 149)
Domaine Anthea Merlot, Vin de Pays d'Oc 1990 (page 143)
Domaine de Picheral Rouge, Vin de Pays d'Oc 1989 (page 147)
Domaine de Picheral Syrah, Vin de Pays d'Oc 1989 (page 147)
Château de Caraguilhes, Corbières, 1988 (page 141)
Château la Maubastit, Bordeaux Supérieur 1988 (page 130)

Sainsbury (selected stores)

J.Sainsbury plc, Stamford House, Stamford Street, London SE1 9LL. Tel. 071 921 6000

White

St Ursula Rivaner QmP 1989 halbtrocken (page 111)

Red

Domaine St Apollinaire Côtes du Rhône 1988 (page 155)
   Also listed as an organic wine is Domaine Coursay-Village, Muscadet, which we do not consider as suitable for inclusion in this list because there is insufficient evidence that it is in fact organically produced.

Tesco

Tesco Stores plc, Tesco House, Delamare Road, Cheshunt, Waltham Cross, Herts EN8 9SL. Tel. 0992 32222

Red
Château de Caraguilhes, Corbières 1988 (page 141)

Waitrose (80 plus stores mainly in the south)

Waitrose, Doncastle Road, Southern Industrial Area, Bracknell, Herts RG12 4XA. Tel. 0344 424680

Red
Château de Prade Bordeaux Supérieur 1988 (page 130)

William Morrisons (50 stores in the North and Midlands)

William Morrisons, Junction 41 Industrial Estate, Wakefield, West Yorks. Tel. 0924 870000

Red
Domaine de Picheral Merlot/Syrah, Vin de Pays d'Oc 1989 (page 147)

8

INDEPENDENT RETAILERS

The following is by no means an exhaustive list of all of the shops that sell organic wine. Those that are included stock a fair range but if you know of a shop that should be included, do write and let us know. Telephone numbers are included where known.

Avon
Real Food Supplies, 36C Gloucester Road, Bishopston, Bristol, BS7 8AR. Tel. 0272 232015
Seasons, 10 George Street, Bath, Avon
Widcombe Wine, 12 Widcombe Parade, Claverton Street, Bath, Avon

Berks
Oasis Wholefoods, 96 Peascod Street, Windsor, Berks, SL4 1DH. Tel. 0753 860618

Bucks
Only Natural, 41 St Peter's Court, Chalfont St Peter, Bucks, SL9 9QQ. Tel. 0753 889441

Cornwall
Carley and Co, 34-36 St Austell Street, Truro, Cornwall, TR1 1SE. Tel. 0872 77686

Cumbria
The Village Bakery, Melmerby, Nr Penrith, Cumbria. Tel. 076881 515

Derbyshire

Beanos Wholefoods, Holme Road, Matlock Bath, Derbyshire, DE4 3NU. Tel. 0629 57130
Whitakers Wines, 8 Market Place, Buxton, Derbyshire, SK17 6EB. Tel. 0298 70241

Devon

Elliots Farm Shop and Nursery, Offwell, Honiton, Devon, EX14 9RT. Tel. 040483 549
Food on the Hill, 5A Mill Street, Ottery St Mary, Devon, EX11 1AB. Tel. 0404 812109
The Wine Centre, Russell Street, Tavistock, Devon, PL19 8BD

Durham

Durham Community Co-op, 85A New Elvet, Durham, Co Durham. Tel. 09138 61183

Gloucestershire

The Organic Shop, The Square, Stow-on-the-Wold, Cheltenham, Glos, GL54 1AB. Tel. 0451 31004

Hampshire

Naturally Best Foods, 78 Ewell Way, Totton, Southampton, SO4 3PP. Tel. 0703 868384

Hereford and Worcester

Brewers Basics, 15A Broad Street, Leominster, Hereford and Worcester
Hay Wholefoods and Delicatessen, 1 Lion Street, Hay on Wye, Hereford and Worcester, HR3 5AA. Tel. 0497 820708/820388
Only Natural, 99B Church Street, Great Malvern, Hereford and Worcester, WR14 2AE. Tel. 0684 561772

Herts

Cook's Delight, 360-364 High Street, Berkhamsted, Herts, HP4 1HU. Tel. 0442 863584

Lancs

Single Step Co-op Ltd, 78A Penny Street, Lancaster, Lancs LA1 1XN. Tel. 0524 63021

London
The Beer Shop, Pitfield Street, London N1
Bennett and Luck, 54 Islington Park Street, London N1
Bottlenecks, 229 West End Lane, West Hampstead, London NW6
Bumblebee Natural Foods, 30 Brecknock Road, London N7 0DD
Bushwacker Wholefoods, 59 Goldhawk Road, London W12 8EG. Tel. 081 743 2359
Clearspring, 196 Old Street, London EC1
Cornucopia Wholefoods, 64 St Mary's Road, Ealing, London W5 5EX. Tel. 081 579 9431
Cranks Health Foods, 8 Marshall Street, London W1V 1LP. Tel. 071 437 2915
Crystal Palace Wholefoods, 74 Church Road, Crystal Palace, London SE19. Tel. 081 771 4605
Grape Hive Wines, 392a Chiswick High Road, London W4
Haelan Centre, 41 The Broadway, Crouch End, London N8
Natural Foods Ltd, Unit 14, Hainault Road Industrial Estate, Hainault, London E11 1HD. Tel. 081 539 1034
Neals Yard, 21-23 Shorts Gardens, Covent Garden, London WC2. Tel. 071 836 5151
Olivers, 243 Munster Road, London SW6
The Organic Shop, 120 Ferndale Road, Clapham, London SW4. Tel. 071 737 1365
Peaches Health Foods, 143 High Street, Wanstead, London E11
Peppercorn Wholefoods, 2 Heath Street, Hampstead, London NW3. Tel. 071 431 1251
Ravensbourne Wines, Bell House, 49 Greenwich High Road, London SE10
Wholefoods, 24 Paddington Street, London W1M 4DR. Tel. 071 935 3924
Wild Oats, 210 Westbourne Grove, London W7

Manchester
St Anne's Wine Store, 3 St Anne's Road, Chorlton-cum-Hardy, Manchester, M21 2TQ. Tel. 061 881 3901

Merseyside
Cornucopia, 71 Everton Road, Southport, Merseyside, PR8 4BT. Tel. 0704 69020

Notts
Hiziki Wholefood Collective Ltd, 15 Goosegate, Hockley, Nottingham, NG1 1FE. Tel. 0602 505523

Oxon
Fluttons, 110 Walton Street, Oxford, Oxon

Shropshire
Pimhill Produce, Lea Hall, Harmer Hill, Shrewsbury, Shropshire, SY4 3DY. Tel. 0939 290342

Somerset
Good Earth Wholefood Store, 4 Priory Road, Wells, Somerset, BA5 1SY. Tel. 0749 78600

Suffolk
Aspall Cyder, Aspall Hall, Debenham, Suffolk IP14 6PD. Tel. 0728 860510
Hungate Health Store, 4 Hungate, Beccles, Suffolk, NR34 9TL. Tel. 0502 715009
Loaves and Fishes, 52 Thoroughfare, Woodbridge, Suffolk, IP12 1AL. Tel. 03943 85650

Sussex
Beaumont Organic, 363 South Coast Road, Telescombe, Brighton, East Sussex, BN10 7HH. Tel. 0273 585551
Full of Beans, 96-97 High Street, Lewes, East Sussex, BN7 1XH. Tel. 0273 472627
The Granary, Prinkle Farm, Bodle Street, Hailsham, East Sussex, BN27 4UD. Tel. 0323 833541
Infinity Foods Co-operative Ltd, 25 North Road, Brighton, East Sussex, BN1 1YA. Tel. 0273 603563/690116
Pallant Wines, Appledram, Appledram Lane, Chichester, Sussex
Stairs Farm Produce, Stairs Farmhouse, High Street, Hartfield, East Sussex, TN7 4AB. Tel. 089277 793

West Midlands
The Health Food Centre, 20 High Street, Solihull, West Midlands, B91 3TB. Tel. 021 705 0134

Rackhams, Corporation Street, Birmingham, B2 5JS. Tel. 021 200 3333

Ryton Gardens Shop, National Centre for Organic Gardening, Ryton-on-Dunsmore, Coventry, CV8 3LG. Tel. 0203 303517

Yorks
The Dram Shop, 21 Commonside, Sheffield, S6. Tel. 0742 683117
Grain of Sense Wholefoods, 29 Brudenell Road, Hyde Park, Leeds, LS5 1HA. Tel. 0532 757410
Ripley Castle Shop, Ripley, Near Harrogate, N Yorks. Tel. 0423 771465
The Wholefood Shop, 4 Half Moon Street, Huddersfield, West Yorks, HD1 2JJ. Tel. 0484 663301
York Beer Shop, 28 Sandringham Street, York, YO1 4BA. Tel. 0904 647136

Scotland
Real Foods, 37 Broughton Street, Edinburgh, Lothian, EH1 3JU. Tel. 031 557 1911 (Wines also available by mail order)

Wales
The Celtic Vintner, 73 Derwen Fawr Road, Sketty, Swansea, Glamorgan
Van's Good Food Shop, Laburnum House, Middleton Street, Llandrindod Wells, Powys. Tel. 0597 3074
Wholefoods of Newport, Market Street, Newport, Dyfed, SA42 0PH. Tel. 0239 820773

ORGANIC WINE BY MAIL ORDER

The following companies sell wine by mail order. In each case we have included the address, telephone number, and a brief note on their operation, including the terms of trade where known.

A Case of Wine, Twm Tawel, Horeb, Llandysul, Dyfed, SA44 4HY. Tel. 055932 3342

A Case of Wine is a small Welsh-based company offering fine wines from around the world including over 50 organic wines. They specialize in mixed cases and offer a nationwide delivery service.

Dunkertons Cider Company, Hays Head, Luntley, Pembridge, Hereford and Worcester, HR6 9ED. Tel. 05447 653

All ciders are made from genuine cider apples, including many rare such as Bloody Turk and Sheep's Nose. Their perry is made from Merrylegs and Painted Lady — genuine perry pears. No water, colourings or flavourings added.

Goujon & Fils Ltd, 1 Monza Street, Wapping Wall, London E1 9SP. Tel. 071 488 4971, Fax 071 481 3238

Goujon & Fils currently have three organic producers amongst their portfolio of wines and do not sell direct to the public. However, they will be glad to give you details of the retail stockist nearest you.

HDRA (Sales) Ltd, National Centre for Organic Gardening, Ryton-on-Dunsmore, Coventry, CV8 3LG. Tel. 0203 303517, Fax 0203 639229

Access and Visa accepted.

One of the widest ranges of organic wines in the UK is stocked at the Ryton Gardens shop, open seven days a week all year round. Wines are also sent mail order to all locations in mainland UK. All profits from wine sales go to fund the organic research work of the parent body, The Henry Doubleday Research Association.

Haughton Fine Wines, Chorley Green Lane, Chorley, Nantwich, Cheshire CW5 8JR. Tel. 0270 74537, Fax 0270 74233
Voted Northern Wine Merchant of the Year in 1990 by *Wine Magazine* and the *Sunday Telegraph*. 'Haughton cover the organic field with great skill, and deserve a particular commendation for offering a range of the best organic wines in the country' — Robert Joseph, *Good Wine Guide 1990*.

Organics, 290a Fulham Palace Road, London SW6 6HP. Tel. 071 381 9924
Organics specialize in Italian organic wines. French organic wines and natural beers, juices, nectars and tomato products are also included in their list. Mail order (mixed cases) and national wholesale distribution.

The Organic Wine Company Ltd, P O Box 81, High Wycombe, Bucks, HP13 5QN. Tel. 0494 446557, Fax 0494 437926
Access and Visa accepted.
'From Vin de Pays to vintage fine wines, the largest range of organic wines available from one UK source!' So claim this small southern-based company. Mixed cases available. Trade outlets supplied. Tastings by arrangement.

Rodgers Fine Wines, 37 Ben Bank Road, Silkstone Common, Barnsley, South Yorks, S75 4PE. Tel. 0226 790794
Importer supplying trade/public specializing in single vineyard high quality German wines. Available by mail order nationwide.

Sedlescombe Organic Wines, Sedlescombe Vineyard, Roberts-bridge, East Sussex, TN32 5SA. Tel. 058083 715
Produces a range of organic red and white wines to Soil Association standard. Also stocks other organic wines from around the world.

Vinceremos Wines, Unit 10, Ashley Industrial Estate, Wakefield Road, Ossett, West Yorks. Tel. 0924 276393, Fax 0924 276353
Access and Visa accepted.
Nationwide home delivery of any 12 different wines from their huge range of organically produced wines from all over the world. All vegetarian, verified as genuinely organic by independent standards and control organizations. Not only wines but also

juices, beer, ciders, spirits and 'vino palido' (sherry). Trade terms available. Visitors welcome.

Vintage Roots, 25 Manchester Road, Reading, Berks, RG1 3QE. Tel. 0734 662569

One of the country's larger organic wine specialists, their services include a national mail order operation, biannual bin-end sales and promotions. Separate trade list. Spirits, liqueurs, beer and vinegars also available.

Winecellars, 153 Wandsworth High Street, London SW18. Tel. 081 871 3970

Probably the best non-organic Italian wine specialist in the UK, they appear here as stockists of just one organic wine and that's French — Terre Blanche! Retailers rather than mail order suppliers.

Whitakers Wines, 8 Market Place, Buxton, Derbyshire, SK17 6EB. Tel. 0298 70241

Only organic wines sold (by retail, mail order and wholesale). The first totally organic wine retailer in the country. All wines are bought directly from producers who all belong to recognized organic organizations.

Anyone wishing to sample many of the organic wines listed in this book can do no better than visit the Midlands each July for the National Organic Wine Fair. The event is organized by The Henry Doubleday Research Association, Britain's largest organic organization, whose gardens at Ryton, near Coventry, are famous as the setting for the Channel 4 television series 'All Muck and Magic?'. Safeway plc have traditionally sponsored the fair, which is a chance to taste the best in organic wines and also an occasion at which to meet the importers, suppliers and other enthusiasts for a chat! Telephone 0203 303517 for further details.

GLOSSARY

TASTING WORDS

Aromatic: A distinctive and spicy smell.

Astringent: Causes your mouth to pucker up.

Big: A full flavour that fills the mouth; the opposite of light and undemanding.

Biscuity: A flavour of digestive-style biscuits, which can also refer to the yeasty flavour. Usually associated with Champagne, and then because of the Chardonnay grape in the wine.

Body: The fullness of flavour, or lack of it.

Bouquet: The smell.

Buttery: A rich, fat smell or taste, like butter.

Citrus: Usually a smell or flavour of lemons.

Clean: Direct, usually fresh and straightforward flavours.

Correct: A wine that is made in a formally conventional style, without idiosyncrasies or faults.

Creamy: A flavour that is smooth and rich like cream.

Fat: Not too dry with an almost oily character that coats the taste buds.

Fresh: Lively and ripe flavours. Wines, like foods, can go stale in flavour.

Harmonious: Used to describe a wine where all the different elements are well integrated.

Length: The length of time that the flavour remains in the mouth.

Mature: That the particular wine has aged and developed in flavour to a point where it will not change significantly for the better in the future; where it has lost its coarseness.

Nose: The smell.

Petillance: A spritz, very lightly fizzy. Usually found in good Muscadet and some red and white wines made in a particular style.

Round: Well balanced.
Serious: A wine whose flavours are quite demanding and require notice; opposite of light and quaffable.
Steely: Hard, usually in a red wine that will soften up with age.
Upfront: The flavours are immediately obvious.
Weight: The degree to which the flavour seems impressed on the taste buds; often closely related to, but not always the same as, the depth of colour of the wine.
Zesty: An extrovert, lively flavour.

GENERAL TERMS

Appellation Contrôlée: The top rung on the ladder of the French system for regulating production of wines, designed to increase quality.
Auslese: German term for wine made from specially selected late-picked grapes with a high natural sugar content.
Berenauslese: As above, but from individually selected grapes even more concentrated in sugar.
Biodynamic: Method of carrying out activity in conjunction with the influence of the planets.
Blanc de Blancs: White wine made from white grapes. Can apply to any wine.
Bordeaux mixture: Lime and copper sulphate spray used as a preventive measure against rot and mould on vines.
Botrytis: The fungus, known as Noble Rot, that can attack grapes and take out the fluid, leaving very highly concentrated sugar.
Brut: The (French) word for dry, when applied to sparkling wines in France.
Cave: Cellar (French).
Chaptalization: The addition of sugar to the 'must' in order to raise the alcoholic strength of the finished wine.
Claret: English name for red Bordeaux wines.
Contact sprays: Those that are sprayed on to the outside of a plant.
Côte(s) or Coteau(x): Hillside(s) where grapes are grown.
Cru: Literally this means 'growth'. It is usually used with the word 'Classé' — a 'Cru Classé' means a 'classed growth', or property classified as producing particularly high quality wine. (French)
Demi-sec: Medium dry (French).
Denominacion de Origen: The DO is the Spanish quality level equivalent to AC in France.

Denominazione di Origine Controllata (e Garantia): DOC(G) is the Italian equivalent of the French AC.

Doux: Sweet (French)

Eiswein: German term for wine made from grapes picked when frozen on the vine — and with very concentrated sugar.

Fining: The process of adding a substance to fermented wine in order to remove particles and protein haze.

Fortified wines: Made by adding brandy or other grape spirit to a wine, making it higher in alcohol, e.g. Port, Sherry.

Halbtrocken: Medium dry (German).

Hectare: European unit of measurement for vineyards, equivalent to 2.47 acres.

Hectolitre: One hundred litres, equivalent to 133 75cl bottles, or just over 11 12-bottle cases.

Humus: The organic matter found in the soil which provides the necessary nutrients for it to live.

Kabinett: First level of special quality wine in the German quality system, based on the degree of natural sugar in the grape juice.

Macération carbonique: Method of fermenting whole, uncrushed grapes under a layer of carbon dioxide. Produces light, fresh, fruity wines and is the hallmark of Beaujolais.

Malolatic fermentation: Nothing to do with the fermentation that produces alcohol, this is a secondary activity where tart malic acid is converted into softer lactic acid. Desirable in wines that would otherwise be too acidic.

Marc: The pressed skins (and possibly stalks) after fermentation.

Méthode Champenoise: Way of making wine sparkling by a secondary fermentation in the bottle where the carbon dioxide is trapped in the bottle. Made famous in the Champagne region of France.

Micro-climate: Specific conditions in a small area.

Moelleux: Literally 'Mellow', it refers to sweet, usually aperitif style wines (French).

Must: Grape juice prior to its fermentation into wine.

Negociant: Merchant who 'negotiates' — middle man buying and perhaps blending wines for resale.

Noble Rot: See Botrytis

Organically grown: At its simplest, grown without the use of synthetic chemical fertilizers or pesticides.

Oxidation: Process whereby oxygen in the air can affect a wine and, if excessive, turn it sour.

Pheromone: Sexual trap used in organic pest control to lure male insects.

Phylloxera: Beetle that attacks vine roots and destroys them; it ravaged European vineyards in the last century and is now combated by grafting European grape varieties onto resistant American rootstocks.

Qualitätswein Bestimmter Anbaugebiete (QbA): Most common level of quality wine in Germany.

Qualitätswein mit Prädikat (QmP): Quality wine with distinction. Better than QbA, and has the subcategories of Kabinett, Spätlese, etc.

Racking off: The process of syphoning wine off the sediment that has formed while in the vat and storing in a fresh container.

Récolte: Harvest, also used to denote the vintage. (French)

Sec: Dry, for French still wines.

Sekt: German sparkling wine.

Spätlese: Late-picked grapes, more concentrated sugar than Kabinett. (German)

Sulphur dioxide: Otherwise known as SO_2 or E220, the chemical used in virtually all wine production as a sterilizing and preserving agent. Used in very reduced amounts by organic winemakers. Smells and tastes metallic, and is one of the principal causes of hangovers.

Systemic: Liquid, usually an insecticide, which works by being absorbed into the internal system of a plant.

Tannin: Found in the stalks and pips of the grape. It creates a mouth-puckering, teeth-furring sensation when found to excess in a wine. An essential element in enabling red wines to mature and develop over time, it smoothens and diminishes with age.

Tartrates: Harmless crystals formed from tartaric acid. Found naturally in wine, usually when the liquid is subject to cold temperatures.

Trocken: Dry (German).

Trockenberenauslese: German category for wine made from individually selected late-picked grapes affected by Noble Rot. Very high sugar concentration capable of producing fantastically rich and sweet wines.

Varietal: 'New World' term for grape variety.

Vendange: Harvest (French).

Vendange tardive: Late harvest, usually grapes making concentrated rich wines. (French)

Ver de la grappe: Caterpillar that attacks vine leaves and is a major pest. (French)

Vin Delimité de Qualité Supérieure (VDQS): Not very widely used, a quality level lower than AC. (French)

Vin de Pays: Also lower than AC, a less strict but also regional category, literally 'country wine'. (French)

Vin de Table: And its equivalent in other countries (Vino da Tavola, etc.) means unregulated wine from anywhere in the country. The most basic category.

Vinification: The techniques employed in turning grapes into wine.

Vintage: The year in which the grapes that made the wine were harvested.

Viticulture: Growing vines and producing grapes.

FURTHER READING AND RESOURCES

FURTHER READING

A very wide range of books about many aspects of wine is now available, covering different countries, regions, grape types, styles of wine, food and wine, the history of wine and so forth. There are also several publications dealing with different aspects of organic growing, and many more that deal with general environmental issues.

Magazines and Periodicals

Decanter, Priory House, 8 Battersea Park Road, London SW8 4BG. Tel. 071 627 8181

Which? Wine Monthly, Consumers' Association, P O Box 44, Hertford, SG14 1SH. Tel. 0992 587773

Wine Magazine, 60 Waldegrave Road, Teddington, Middlesex, TW11 8LG. Tel. 081 943 5943

Books

Barr, A. *Wine Snobbery* (Faber and Faber, 1988)

British Medical Association *Pesticides, Chemicals and Health* (BMA, 1990)

Deschamps, S. *Les Secrets des Bons Vins Naturels* (La Vie Naturelle)

Fielden, C. *Is this the Wine you Ordered, Sir?* (Christopher Helm, 1989)

Hanssen, M. *The New E for Additives* (Thorsons, 1987)

Johnson, H. *Pocket Wine Book* (Mitchell Beazley, 1989)

Johnson, H. *The World Atlas of Wine,* 3rd Edition (Mitchell Beazley, 1989)

London Food Commission *Food Adulteration and How to Beat it* (Unwin, 1988)

Mabey, D., Gear A. and J. *Thorsons Organic Consumer Guide* (Thorsons, 1990)

Mitchell, C. and Wright, I. *The Organic Wine Guide* (Mainstream, 1987)

Parratt, T. *Name your Poison* (Robert Hale, 1990)

Robinson, J. *Vines, Grapes and Wines* (Mitchell Beazley, 1986)

Sutcliffe, S. *The Wine Drinker's Handbook* (Pan, 1985)

ORGANIZATIONS

Henry Doubleday Research Association
Ryton Gardens, Ryton-on-Dunsmore, Coventry, CV8 3LG
Tel. 0203 303517

Britain's largest organization concerned with organic growing. As a registered charity its main purpose is to research, demonstrate and promote environmentally safe techniques. HDRA now has around 18,000 members who receive a quarterly newsletter, and have free access to Ryton Gardens at the National Centre for Organic Gardening. The Association is involved in many projects, ranging from the conservation of old seed varieties to tree-planting schemes in the Third World. It publishes numerous leaflets and books, and provides an advisory service, as well as stocking a wide range of equipment for the organic gardener, books, organic foods and one of the widest ranges of organic wines in the UK. Also runs an organic mail order company, HDRA (Sales).

The Soil Association
86 Colston Street, Bristol, Avon, BS1 5BB
Tel. 0272 290661

The Soil Association is a registered charity, founded in 1946 to promote the organic philosophy. Its symbol scheme licenses commercial food production to the highest organic standards. The Soil Association has around 5,000 members, and membership services include a quarterly journal, *The Living Earth*, a network of local groups and an information service.

British Organic Farmers and The Organic Growers Association (BOF/OGA)
86 Colston Street, Bristol, Avon, BS1 5BB
Tel. 0272 299666/299600

Britain's producer association, representing over 1,000 organic producers throughout the British Isles. Membership services include a quarterly journal, *The New Farmer and Grower*, a national programme of farm walks, an information service, conferences and seminars. It also runs courses in association with the Agricultural Training Board. A regional group network covers most of the UK. An associated company supplies printed bags, boxes and other packaging materials to organic producers.

International Federation of Organic Agriculture Movements (IFOAM)

c/o Ockozentrum Imsbach, D-6695 Tholey-Theley, Germany
Tel. 068 535190 (From the UK, dial 010 49 then omit initial 0).

The global forum for organic organizations, with 230 members worldwide. Organizes scientific and other international conferences. Responsible for producing standards for organic agriculture that are the basis for national standards.

Elm Farm Research Centre (EFRC)

Hamstead Marshall, Nr Newbury, Berkshire, RG15 0HR.
Tel. 0488 58298

A charitable organization carrying out independent research into organic agriculture at its 232-acre farm and at other sites around the country. Runs the Organic Advisory Service — a consultancy covering conversion planning, telephone enquiries, visits to established organic farms and soil analysis. Publishes a range of technical books and booklets.

The Irish Organic Farmers and Growers Association (IOFGA)

Springmount, Ballyboughal, Co. Dublin.

Responsible for administering organic standards in the Republic of Ireland. IOFGA has close links with the Soil Association, it administers the independent Irish symbol scheme and has its own logo. Contact: Nicky Kyle.

Parents for Safe Food

Britannia House, 1-11 Glenthorne Road, London W6 0LF

Formed in 1989 by actress Pamela Stephenson and other celebrities to campaign against the use of Alar in apples. Plans to widen the debate by looking at other food contaminants.

The Pesticide Trust

20 Compton Terrace, London N1 2UN
Tel. 071 354 3860

Formed in 1988 to create awareness among decision-makers over the use and regulation of pesticides; to alert workers and consumers to the problems associated with pesticides, and to promote alternatives to present pesticide policies in developed and developing countries. Publishes *Pesticide News* quarterly, and plans to publish other handbooks and newsletters in the future.

APPENDIX 1:
WINE DEVELOPMENT BOARD GUIDE CODES

WHITE WINE GUIDE CODES

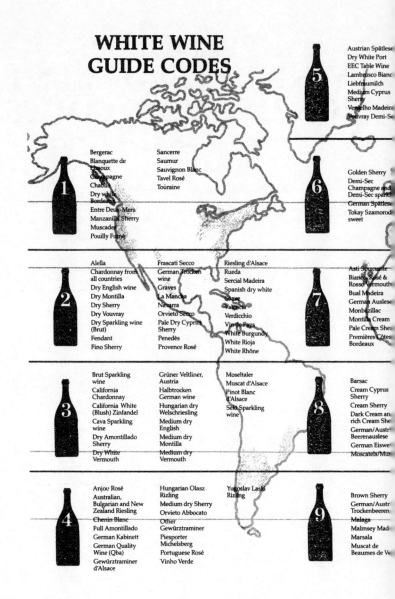

5
Austrian Spätlese
Dry White Port
EEC Table Wine
Lambrusco Bianco
Liebfraumilch
Medium Cyprus
Sherry
Verdelho Madeira
Vouvray Demi-Se

1
Bergerac
Blanquette de
Limoux
Champagne
Chablis
Dry white
Bordeaux
Entre Deux-Mers
Manzanilla Sherry
Muscadet
Pouilly Fumé

Sancerre
Saumur
Sauvignon Blanc
Tavel Rosé
Touraine

6
Golden Sherry
Demi-Sec
Champagne and
Demi-Sec sparkl
German Spätlese
Tokay Szamorod
sweet

2
Alella
Chardonnay from
all countries
Dry English wine
Dry Montilla
Dry Sherry
Dry Vouvray
Dry Sparkling wine
(Brut)
Fendant
Fino Sherry

Frascati Secco
German Trocken
wine
Graves
La Mancha
Navarra
Orvieto Secco
Pale Dry Cyprus
Sherry
Penedès
Provence Rosé

Riesling d'Alsace
Rueda
Sercial Madeira
Spanish dry white
Soave
Valencia
Verdicchio
Vin de Pays
White Burgundy
White Rioja
White Rhône

7
Asti Spumante
Bianco, Rosé &
Rosso Vermouth
Bual Madeira
German Auslese
Monbazillac
Montilla Cream
Pale Cream She
Premières Côtes
Bordeaux

3
Brut Sparkling
wine
California
Chardonnay
California White
(Blush) Zinfandel
Cava Sparkling
wine
Dry Amontillado
Sherry
Dry White
Vermouth

Grüner Veltliner,
Austria
Halbtrocken
German wine
Hungarian dry
Welschriesling
Medium dry
English
Medium dry
Montilla
Medium dry
Vermouth

Moseltaler
Muscat d'Alsace
Pinot Blanc
d'Alsace
Sekt Sparkling
wine

8
Barsac
Cream Cyprus
Sherry
Cream Sherry
Dark Cream an
rich Cream She
German/Austr
Beerenauslese
German Eiswe
Moscatels/Mus

4
Anjou Rosé
Australian,
Bulgarian and New
Zealand Riesling
Chenin Blanc
Full Amontillado
German Kabinett
German Quality
Wine (Qba)
Gewürztraminer
d'Alsace

Hungarian Olasz
Rizling
Medium dry Sherry
Orvieto Abbocato
Other
Gewürztraminer
Piesporter
Michelsberg
Portuguese Rosé
Vinho Verde

Yugoslav Laski
Rizling

9
Brown Sherry
German/Austr
Trockenbeeren
Malaga
Malmsey Mad
Marsala
Muscat de
Beaumes de Ve

RED WINE
GUIDE CODES

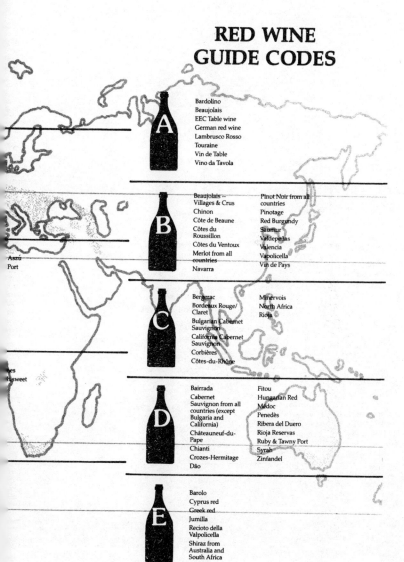

A
Bardolino
Beaujolais
EEC Table wine
German red wine
Lambrusco Rosso
Touraine
Vin de Table
Vino da Tavola

B
Beaujolais –
Villages & Crus
Chinon
Côte de Beaune
Côtes du
Roussillon
Côtes du Ventoux
Merlot from all
countries
Navarra

Pinot Noir from all
countries
Pinotage
Red Burgundy
Saumur
Valdepeñas
Valencia
Valpolicella
Vin de Pays

C
Bergerac
Bordeaux Rouge/
Claret
Bulgarian Cabernet
Sauvignon
California Cabernet
Sauvignon
Corbières
Côtes-du-Rhône

Minervois
North Africa
Rioja

D
Bairrada
Cabernet
Sauvignon from all
countries (except
Bulgaria and
California)
Châteauneuf-du-
Pape
Chianti
Crozes-Hermitage
Dão

Fitou
Hungarian Red
Médoc
Penedès
Ribera del Duero
Rioja Reservas
Ruby & Tawny Port
Syrah
Zinfandel

E
Barolo
Cyprus red
Greek red
Jumilla
Recioto della
Valpolicella
Shiraz from
Australia and
South Africa

INDEX

SUBJECT INDEX

This index refers to material in Part I of the book. Wines are listed in a separate wine index.

INDEX TO WINE LISTINGS

With a few exceptions, wines and other products are listed by general type, usually a geographical region eg Bordeaux, Vin de pays; or a grape name eg Chardonnay, Kerner.

For example:
Chateau Balluemondon Bordeaux Moelleux 1988/90
see: Bordeaux
        Moelleux 89, 91

READERS' COMMENTS

To: Thorsons Organic Wine Guide
Thorsons
HarperCollins*Publishers*
77-85 Fulham Palace Road
Hammersmith
London W6 8JB

Use this form to comment on any supplier or retail outlet worthy
of notice or on any organic wines you would like to tell us about.

Name of establishment_____

Address_____

_____

_____

_____Postcode_____

Telephone No. (if known)_____

Type of business (e.g. wholefood shop, farm, restaurant)

_____

_____

_____